T0032063

Wildflowers
of the Carolinas
Field Guide

Nora and Rick Bowers
Stan Tekiela

Adventure Publications
Cambridge, Minnesota

Dedication

To my sister, Beth, for sharing her love of flowers with me—Nora

To Matt Johnson, who always kept plants on my mind and taught me so much about them—Rick

To my daughter, Abigail Rose. The sweetest flower in my life—Stan

Acknowledgments

Nora and Rick thank the following people for their generosity and support, without which this book would not have been possible: Steve and Jo Blanich, Dave and Debbie Ellsworth, Ernestine and Dennis Lawrence, Kim and Cindy Risen, and Stan Tekiela.

A very special thanks to the following people and institutions who shared their knowledge of plants with us: Daniel Moerman for the Native American Ethnobotany website, University of Michigan-Dearborn; Dan Tenaglia for his plant identification website at www.alabamaplants.com; Alan S. Weakley for making his *Flora of the Carolinas, Virginia, Georgia, and Surrounding Areas* available online; Laura White at Stevens Nature Center, Cary, North Carolina; the Flora of North America website; University of North Carolina Herbarium; and North Carolina Botanical Garden at Chapel Hill.

Edited by Deborah Walsh

Technical Editor: Jaret C. Daniels

Cover, book design and illustrations by Jonathan Norberg

Cover photo: Spiderwort by **RukiMedia/Shutterstock.com**
All photos copyright of their respective photographers.

Tom Barnes/University of Kentucky: 156, 318, 380, 392; **Steven J. Baskauf:** 188, 312 (fruit inset), 378; **Bob Bierman:** 50; **Ted Bodner/Southern Science Society/Bugwood.org:** 78, 134, 330; **Rick & Nora Bowers:** 36, 38, 60 (both), 104, 120, 142, 150, 176, 180 (fruit inset), 218, 228, 234 (main), 242, 262, 274, 290, 304, 316, 324, 332, 334, 364, 366, 394, 396, 410, 414 (both);

Photo credits continued on page 430

10 9 8 7 6 5 4 3 2 1

Wildflowers of the Carolinas Field Guide
First Edition 2008, Second Edition 2022
Copyright © 2008 and 2022 by Nora Mays Bowers, Rick Bowers and Stan Tekiela
Published by Adventure Publications
An imprint of AdventureKEEN
310 Garfield Street South
Cambridge, Minnesota 55008
(800) 678-7006
www.adventurepublications.net
All rights reserved
Printed in the United States of America
ISBN 978-1-64755-221-3 (pbk.); ISBN 978-1-64755-222-0 (ebook)

TABLE OF CONTENTS

Introduction

Sample Pages

The Wildflowers

THE CAROLINAS AND WILDFLOWERS

The Carolinas are great places for wildflower enthusiasts! From the coastal plain in the east to the Appalachian Mountains in the west, this means the Carolinas are fortunate to have an extremely diverse, often unique and a very healthy variety of wonderful wildflowers.

Wildflowers of the Carolinas Field Guide is an easy-to-use field guide to help the curious nature seeker identify 200 of the most common and widespread wildflowers in North and South Carolina. It features, with several exceptions, the herbaceous wildflowers of the Carolinas. Herbaceous plants have green soft stems and die back to the ground each autumn. Only a few plants with woody stems have been included, because these particular plants are very common and have large showy flowers.

STRATEGIES FOR IDENTIFYING WILDFLOWERS

Determining the color of the flower is the first step in a simple five-step process to identify a wildflower.

Because this guide is organized by color, identifying an unknown wildflower is as simple as matching the color of the flower to the color section of the book. The color tabs on each page identify the color section.

The second step in determining the identity of a wildflower is the size. Within each color section, the flowers are arranged by the size of the flower, or flower cluster, from small to large. A plant with a single, small, yellow flower will be in the beginning of the yellow section while a large white flower will be toward the end of the white section. Sometimes flowers are made up of many individual flowers in clusters that are perceived to be one larger flower. Therefore, these will be ordered by the size of the cluster, not the individual flower. See page 432 for rulers to help estimate flower and leaf size.

Once you have determined the color and approximate size, observe the appearance of the flower. Is it a single flower or cluster of flowers? If it is a cluster, is the general shape of the cluster flat, round or spike? For the single flowers, note if the flower has a regular, irregular, bell or tube shape. Also, counting the number of petals might help to identify these individual flowers. Compare your findings with the descriptions on each page. Examining the flower as described above should result in narrowing the identity of the wildflower down to just a few candidates.

The fourth step is to look at the leaves. There are several possible shapes or types of leaves. Simple leaves have only one leaf blade but can be lobed. Compound leaves have a long central leaf stalk with many smaller leaflets attached. Twice compound leaves have two or more leaf stalks and many leaflets. Sometimes it is helpful to note if the leaves have toothed or smooth margins (edges), so look for this also.

For the fifth step, check to see how the leaf is attached to the stem. Some plants may look similar but have different leaf attachments so this can be very helpful. Look to see if the leaves are attached opposite of each other along the stem, alternately, or whorled around a point on the stem. Sometimes the leaves occur at the base of the plant (basal). Some leaves do not have a leaf stalk and clasp the stem at their base (clasping) and in some cases the stem appears to pass through the base of the leaf (perfoliate).

Using these five steps (color, size, shape, leaves and leaf attachment) will help you gather the clues needed to quickly and easily identify the common wildflowers of the Carolinas.

USING THE ICONS

Sometimes the botanical terms for leaf type, attachment and type of flower can be confusing and difficult to remember. Because of this, we have included icons at the bottom of each page. They can be used to quickly and visually match the main features of the plant to the specimen you are viewing without even needing to completely understand the botanical terms. By using the photos, text descriptions and icons in this field guide, you should be able to quickly and easily identify most of the common wildflowers of the Carolinas.

The icons are arranged from left to right in the following order: flower cluster type, flower type, leaf type, leaf attachment and fruit. The first two flower icons refer to cluster type and flower type. While these are not botanically separate categories, we have made separate icons for them to simplify identification.

Flower Cluster Icons

 (icon color is dependent on flower color)

Flat   Round   Spike

Any cluster (tightly formed group) of flowers can be categorized into one of three cluster types based on its over-all shape. The flat, round and spike types refer to the cluster shape, which is easy to observe. Technically there is another cluster type, composite, which appears as a single daisy-like flower but is actually a cluster of many tiny flowers. Because this is often perceived as a flower type, we have included the icon in the flower type section. See page 9 for its description.

Some examples of cluster types

Flat   **Round**   **Spike**

Flower Type Icons

Regular   Irregular   Bell   Tube   Composite

(icon color is dependent on flower color)

Botanically speaking, there are many types of flowers, but in this guide, we are simplifying them to five basic types. Regular flowers are defined as having a round shape with three or more petals, lacking a disk-like center. Irregular flowers are not round but uniquely shaped with fused petals. Bell flowers are hanging with fused petals. Tube flowers are longer and narrower than bell flowers and point up. Composite flowers (technically a flower cluster) are usually round compact clusters of tiny flowers appearing as one larger flower.

Some examples of flower types

Regular   Irregular   Bell

Tube   Composite

disk flowers
ray flowers

Composite cluster: Although a composite flower is technically a type of flower cluster, we are including the icon in the flower type category since most people not familiar with botany would consider it as a flower type, not a flower cluster. A composite flower consists of petals (ray flowers) and/or a round disk-like center (disk flowers). Sometimes a flower has only ray flowers, sometimes only disk flowers or both.

Leaf Type Icons

Simple | Simple Lobed | Compound | Twice Compound | Palmate

Leaf type can be broken down into two main types; simple and compound. Simple leaves are leaves that are in one piece; the leaf is not divided into smaller leaflets. It can have teeth or be smooth along the edges. The simple leaf is depicted by the simple leaf icon. Simple leaves may have lobes and sinuses that give the leaf a unique shape. These simple leaves with lobes are depicted by the simple lobed icon.

Some examples of leaf types

Simple | Simple Lobed | Compound

Twice Compound | Palmate

Compound leaves have two or more distinct, small leaves called leaflets that arise from a single stalk. In this field guide we are dividing compound leaves into regular compound, twice compound or palmately compound leaves. Twice compound leaves are those that have many distinct leaflets arising from a secondary leaf stalk. Palmately compound leaves are those with three or more leaflets arising from a common central point.

Leaf Attachment Icons

Alternate Opposite Whorl Clasping Perfoliate Basal

Leaves attach to the stems in different ways. There are six main types of attachment, but a plant can have two different types of attachments. This is most often seen in the combination of basal leaves and leaves that attach along the main stem either alternate or opposite (cauline leaves). These wildflowers have some leaves at the base of the plant, usually in a rosette pattern, and some leaves along the stem. In these cases, both icons are included; for most plants, there will only be one leaf attachment icon.

Some examples of leaf attachment

Alternate   **Opposite**   **Whorl**

Clasping   **Perfoliate**   **Basal**

Alternate leaves attach to the stem in an alternating pattern while opposite leaves attach to the stem directly opposite from each other. Whorled leaves have three or more leaves that attach around the stem at the same point. Clasping leaves have no stalk and the base of the leaf partly surrounds the main stem. Perfoliate leaves are also stalkless and have a leaf base that completely surrounds the main stem. Basal leaves are those that originate at the base of a plant, near the ground, usually grouped in a round rosette.

Fruit Icons

 (icon color is dependent on berry or pod color)

Berry   Pod

In some flower descriptions a fruit category has been included. This may be especially useful when a plant is not in bloom or when the fruit is particularly large or otherwise noteworthy. Botanically speaking, there are many types of fruit. We have simplified these often confusing fruit categories into two general groups, berry and pod.

Some examples of fruit types

Berry   **Pod**

The berry icon is used to depict a soft, fleshy, often round structure containing seeds. The pod icon is used to represent a dry structure that, when mature, splits open to release seeds.

BLOOMING SEASON

Most wildflowers have a specific season of blooming. For example, you probably won't see the common spring-blooming Spring Beauty blooming in summer or fall. Knowing the season of bloom can help you narrow your selection as you try to identify an unknown flower. In this field guide, spring usually means March, April and May. Summer refers to the last half of June, July and August. Fall usually means September and October.

LIFE CYCLE/ORIGIN

The life cycle of a wildflower describes how long a wildflower lives. Annual wildflowers are short-lived. They sprout, grow and bloom in only one season, never to return except from seed. Most wildflowers have perennial life cycles that last many years. Perennial wildflowers are usually deeply rooted plants that grow from the roots each year. They return each year from their roots, but they also produce seeds to start other perennial plants. Similar to the annual life cycle is the biennial cycle. This group of plants takes two seasons of growth to bloom. The first year the plant produces a low growth of basal leaves. During the second year, the plant sends up a flower stalk from which it produces seeds, from which new plants can be started. However, the original plant will not return for a third year of growth.

Origin indicates whether the plants are native or non-native. Most of the wildflowers in this book originate in the Carolinas and are considered native plants. Non-native plants were often unintentionally introduced when they escaped from gardens or farms. Most non-native plants are now naturalized in North and South Carolina.

Some plants are also considered invasive (nonnative and capable of destructive spread) or noxious (detrimental to the environment, people or economy). Learn more about the problem plants and other invasives in the Carolinas by visiting the following resources:

South Carolina
South Carolina Plant Pest List, www.clemson.edu/invasives
North Carolina
North Carolina Invasive Plant Council, http://nc-ipc.weebly
.com/nc-invasive-plants.html

HABITATS

Some wildflowers thrive only in specific habitats. They may require certain types of soil, moisture, pH levels, fungi or nutrients. Other wildflowers are generalists and can grow just about anywhere. Sometimes noting the habitat surrounding the flower in question can be a clue to its identity.

RANGE

The wide variety of habitats in the Carolinas naturally restricts the range of certain wildflowers that have specific requirements. Sometimes this section can help you eliminate a wildflower from consideration just based on its range. However, please keep in mind that the ranges indicated are general notations on where the flower is commonly found. They are general guidelines only and there will certainly be exceptions to these ranges.

NOTES

The Notes are fun and fact-filled with many gee-whiz tidbits of interesting information such as historical uses, other common names, insect relationship, color variations and much more. Much of the information in this section cannot be found in other wildflower field guides.

CAUTION

In the Notes, it is mentioned that in some cultures, some of the wildflowers were used for medicine or food. While some find this interesting, DO NOT use this guide to identify edible or medicinal plants. Some of the wildflowers in the Carolinas are toxic or have toxic look-alikes that can cause severe problems. Do not take the chance of making a mistake. Please enjoy the wildflowers with your eyes or camera. In addition, please don't pick, trample or transplant any wildflowers you see. The flower of a plant is its reproductive structure, and if you pick a flower you have eliminated its ability to reproduce.

Transplanting wildflowers is another destructive occurrence. Most wildflowers need specific soil types, pH levels or special bacteria or fungi in the soil to grow properly. If you attempt to transplant a wildflower to a habitat that is not suitable for its particular needs, the wildflower most likely will die. Also, some wildflowers, due to their dwindling populations, are protected by laws that forbid you to harm the plants in any way. The good news is many of our wildflowers in North and South Carolina are now available at local garden centers. These wildflowers have been cultivated and have not been dug from the wild. More gardeners are taking advantage of the availability of these wildflowers, planting native species and helping the planet.

Enjoy the Wild Wildflowers!

Nora, Rick and Stan

Common Name

Scientific name

Color Indicator —

Family: plant family name

Height: average range of mature plant

Flower: general description, type of flower, size of flower, number of petals

Leaf: general description, size, leaf type, type of attachment, toothed or smooth

Fruit: berry or pod

Bloom: spring, summer, fall

Cycle/Origin: annual, perennial, biennial, native, non–native

Habitat: general environment in which you are likely to find the flower

Range: an approximate range where the flower is found

Stan's Notes: helpful identification information, history, origin and other interesting, "gee-whiz" nature facts

Not all icons are found on every page. See preceding pages for icon descriptions.

CLUSTER TYPE   FLOWER TYPE   LEAF TYPE   LEAF ATTACHMENT   FRUIT
Spike   **Irregular**   **Palmate**   **Basal**   **Pod**

Narrowleaf Blue-eyed Grass

Sisyrinchium angustifolium

Family: Iris (Iridaceae)

Height: 4–20" (10–50 cm)

Flower: blue, ½" (1 cm) wide, 6 petals, each notched and tipped with tiny point, bright yellow center; group of flowers on short stalk from longer leaf-like stem

Leaf: thin and grass-like, up to 2" (5 cm) long, bright green, pointed; leaves and flattened winged flower stalks often confused with blades of grass

Fruit: spherical green pod, turning reddish brown or purplish black, ¼" (.6 cm) wide, lengthwise grooves score outside skin into 4 parts

Bloom: spring, summer

Cycle/Origin: perennial; native

Habitat: wet soils, meadows, roadsides, open moist woods, stream banks, swamp edges, sun

Range: throughout

Notes: One of over 40 species of blue-eyed grass in North America, this plant is the most common of several species in the Carolinas. Easily mistaken for clumps of grass when not in bloom, but actually belongs to the Iris family. Has six similar petals and sepals that are shallowly notched and have tiny tips. Stems can be bluish purple. Unlike other irises, which spread by horizontal rhizomes, this primitive iris has fibrous vertical roots.

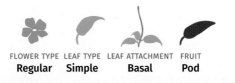

FLOWER TYPE **Regular** LEAF TYPE **Simple** LEAF ATTACHMENT **Basal** FRUIT **Pod**

Azure Bluet
Houstonia caerulea

Family: Madder (Rubiaceae)

Height: 2–4" (5–10 cm)

Flower: pale blue (sometimes sky blue to bluish lavender or white), ½" (1 cm) wide, 4 petals fused into a short tube and then flared out around a bright yellow center; each erect delicate-looking flower on single stalk

Leaf: oval, ½" (1 cm) long, purplish red to green, basally and oppositely attached to reddish stem; 1–2 pair of stalkless upper leaves are much smaller

Bloom: spring, summer

Cycle/Origin: perennial; native

Habitat: acid soils, moist sandy banks, rocky streamsides, open woods, meadows, forest edges, lawns

Range: throughout

Notes: Also known as Quaker Ladies, this delicate flower is relatively large when compared to the small rosette of leaves from which it grows. Another common bluet in the Carolinas, Venus' Pride (pg. 195), has much larger and many more leaves than this plant. Azure Bluet spreads by creeping, mostly underground stems (rhizomes), hence it is found in thick clumps. It makes a great ground cover in shady spots in gardens and lawns. Look for this wildflower in March and April, when daffodils and other spring flowers are blooming in yards.

FLOWER TYPE
Tube

LEAF TYPE
Simple

LEAF ATTACHMENT
Opposite

LEAF ATTACHMENT
Basal

Round-lobed Hepatica
Anemone americana

Family: Buttercup (Ranunculaceae)

Height: 4–6" (10–15 cm)

Flower: pale blue to lavender (can be pink or white), ½–1" (1–2.5 cm) wide, composed of 5–9 petal-like sepals with 3 green bracts underneath; sits on a single hairy stalk that may droop

Leaf: lobed, 1–3" (2.5–7.5 cm) wide, divided into 3 rounded lobes, basally attached to thin hairy stalk

Bloom: spring

Cycle/Origin: perennial; native

Habitat: dry to moist soils that are rich or acid, deciduous woods, sun or shade

Range: western two-thirds of the Carolinas

Notes: One of the springtime ephemerals, Round-lobed Hepatica retains its leaves all winter and quickly sends up flowers each spring before the trees have a chance to produce leaves and shade it out. Leaves from the previous year are dark purple to brown, while new growth is light green. "Hepatica" in the common name is derived from a Greek word for "liver," referring to the lobed leaves that resemble the three lobes of a liver. Because of this, early herbalists erroneously thought the plant was good for treating liver troubles. Also called Liverleaf. The stems of pollinated flowers lengthen and droop near to the ground, allowing easy access for ants to collect and disperse the seeds.

FLOWER TYPE
Regular

LEAF TYPE
Simple Lobed

LEAF ATTACHMENT
Basal

Violet Wood Sorrel

Oxalis violacea

Family: Wood Sorrel (Oxalidaceae)

Height: 4–8" (10–20 cm)

Flower: bluish violet (sometimes all white), ¾" (2 cm) wide, made up of 5 flaring petals; erect flower atop its own stalk; flower stalk rises above the leaves

Leaf: compound, 1½" (4 cm) wide, made up of 3 heart-shaped leaflets; each leaflet, ¾" (2 cm) wide, green or with reddish spots above, maroon below; leaves on reddish purple leafstalks, 4" (10 cm) long, basally attached; leaf resembles a clover leaf

Bloom: spring

Cycle/Origin: perennial; native

Habitat: moist to dry soils, rocky woodlands, riverbanks, grassy borders of forests, clearings, partial shade

Range: throughout

Notes: A delicate plant that lacks stems. The leafstalks and flower stalks, all of which arise from a central underground point, easily break off if disturbed. Flowers are usually bluish violet with a cream-colored base, but can be all white. Spreads by underground runners (rhizomes). Usually found growing in woodland edges. Like other wood sorrels, Violet Wood Sorrel contains oxalic acid, hence the genus name *Oxalis*. The species name *violacea* describes the color of the flowers. Overlaps with the similar-looking invasive Pink Wood Sorrel (*Oxalis debilis*) in South Carolina.

FLOWER TYPE
Regular

LEAF TYPE
Compound

LEAF ATTACHMENT
Basal

Garden Cornflower
Centaurea cyanus

Family: Aster (Asteraceae)

Height: 1–4' (30–122 cm)

Flower: pure blue (sometimes magenta, pink or white) flower head, 1" (2.5 cm) wide, disk flowers only; feathery magenta-tipped green bracts cup the flower head; 1 flower head atop each branch; 25–100 ragged flower heads per plant

Leaf: long and narrow, 5" (13 cm) long, smooth or shallow-toothed margin or with small lobes; alternately attached to green-gray stem streaked with red

Bloom: summer, fall

Cycle/Origin: annual; non-native

Habitat: dry or disturbed soils, pastures, roadsides, sun

Range: throughout

Notes: This frequently cultivated flower is found in wildflower seed mixes and sown along highways by the North Carolina Department of Transportation. A native of the Mediterranean area, it has become invasive. Now found almost everywhere in the United States (especially in the Southeast) where there are disturbed soils, but rare in the mountainous counties of the Carolinas. Ironically, listed as endangered in Great Britain. Also called Bachelor's Button, referring to its use in Old England by single women to signal marital availability. American Goldfinches love the ripe seeds. Treasured for its rare pure blue color and often used in dried flower arrangements.

FLOWER TYPE LEAF TYPE LEAF ATTACHMENT
Composite **Simple** **Alternate**

Common Blue Violet
Viola sororia

Family: Violet (Violaceae)

Height: 4–10" (10–25 cm)

Flower: deep blue or deep violet to lavender (can be white), 1" (2.5 cm) wide, 5 distinct petals surrounding a white center with the 3 lower petals strongly veined; flower usually below leaves on its own flower stalk

Leaf: characteristically heart-shaped, 2–4" (5–10 cm) wide, scalloped teeth, woolly surface, rolled edges, basally attached on woolly stalk

Fruit: cylindrical brown pod with many tiny brown seeds

Bloom: spring

Cycle/Origin: perennial; native

Habitat: disturbed soils, wet or moist woodlands, gardens, partial shade

Range: throughout

Notes: There are some 60 species of violet in the United States and over 500 worldwide. Many botanists now lump together many previously divided violet species under the single species name *sororia*. Looks very similar to the other blue or purple violets, and like all violets, the flower color is highly variable. Often "pops up" in shady gardens and in lawns. Spreads mostly by underground runners, but also by seed. Leaves are high in vitamins and have been used in salads or cooked as greens. A host plant for fritillary butterflies.

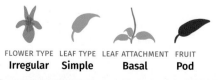

FLOWER TYPE
Irregular

LEAF TYPE
Simple

LEAF ATTACHMENT
Basal

FRUIT
Pod

Common Selfheal
Prunella vulgaris

Family: Mint (Lamiaceae)

Height: 6–12" (15–30 cm)

Flower: thick compact spike cluster, 1–2" (2.5–5 cm) long, of blue-violet-to-pink flowers; each flower, ½" (1 cm) long, made up of 2 petals (lips); upper lip forms a "hood" over fringed, paler blue lower lip

Leaf: lance-shaped, 1–3" (2.5–7.5 cm) long, toothless, on short stalk; oppositely attached leaves sometimes have tiny wing-like leaves growing from point of attachment (node); erect 4-angled stem; multiple unbranched stems from base

Bloom: spring, summer, fall

Cycle/Origin: perennial; non-native

Habitat: wet soils, disturbed areas, pastures, lawns, fields, along roads, bottomland forests, sun to light shade

Range: throughout

Notes: Also known as Selfheal or Heal-all. It is used in folk medicine by many cultures throughout the world. Most commonly used in throat remedies and, lately, for herpes and skin lesions. Preferring light shade, Selfheal will grow in large patches in lawns and adapt to being mowed to a height of 2 inches (5 cm). Like most other members of the Mint family, Selfheal has a square stem, opposing leaves and emits a faint aroma when crushed. The lower lip of the flower acts as a landing platform for insects.

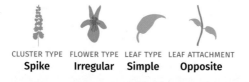

CLUSTER TYPE
Spike

FLOWER TYPE
Irregular

LEAF TYPE
Simple

LEAF ATTACHMENT
Opposite

Bird's Foot Violet

Viola pedata

Family: Violet (Violaceae)

Height: 4–10" (10–25 cm)

Flower: deep to pale blue, purple and white or all white, 1½" (4 cm) wide, 5 distinct petals surrounding a small orange center; colored petals have a lined white throat; lower petals wider than upper; flower usually higher than leaves on its own flower stalk

Leaf: characteristically narrowly lobed, 1–2" (2.5–5 cm) wide, divided into 3 main lobes that resemble a bird's foot; each main lobe is also lobed; each leaf rises from the base of plant on its own leafstalk

Bloom: spring

Cycle/Origin: perennial; native

Habitat: dry rocky or sandy soils, open fields, open woods, partial sun

Range: western two-thirds of the Carolinas

Notes: Bird's Foot Violet looks similar to the Common Blue Violet (pg. 29), but it has larger flowers with petals that are much more irregularly sized and shaped. As with all violets, the color of its flower varies widely. Fortunately, its "bird's foot" leaves make this violet one of the easiest to identify. Look for it growing from cracks in rocks and in dry open fields. Related to the garden pansy, a commonly cultivated annual.

FLOWER TYPE
Irregular

LEAF TYPE
Simple Lobed

LEAF ATTACHMENT
Basal

Spiderwort

Tradescantia occidentalis

Family: Spiderwort (Commelinaceae)

Height: 10–24" (25–61 cm)

Flower: blue to rose (can be pink to white), 1–2" (2.5–5 cm) wide, 3 petals around a golden yellow center; found in clusters of up to 10 flowers; flowers open a few at a time

Leaf: grass-like, 15" (38 cm) long, folded lengthwise to form a V-shaped groove, clasping the stem

Bloom: spring, summer

Cycle/Origin: perennial; native

Habitat: moist or dry soils, sandy ridges, river bottomlands, disturbed sites, meadows, roadsides, sun

Range: throughout

Notes: An unusual-looking plant with exotic-looking flowers, which open in the morning and often wilt by noon on hot days. "Spider" comes from several characteristics unique to the plant, including the angular leaf attachment (suggestive of the legs of a sitting spider) and the stringy mucilaginous sap that strings out like a spider's web when the leaf is torn apart. "Wort" is from *wyrt,* Old English for "plant." Genus name *Tradescantia* is for J. Tradescant, an English gardener. Range overlaps in the western Carolinas with Zigzag Spiderwort *(T. subaspera)* (not shown), which has obvious to somewhat zigzag stems between the alternately attached leaves that are shorter and slightly wider than those of Spiderwort.

FLOWER TYPE	LEAF TYPE	LEAF ATTACHMENT	LEAF ATTACHMENT
Regular	**Simple**	**Alternate**	**Clasping**

Virginia Iris
Iris virginica

Family: Iris (Iridaceae)

Height: 12–36" (30–91 cm)

Flower: pale blue or lavender to pinkish white, 3" (7.5 cm) wide, 3 horizontal drooping sepals with pale yellow streak on white bases, 3 smaller upward-curving petals that are solid-colored; all have dark purple veins; 2–6 flowers on a sometimes branching stalk

Leaf: flat and sword-shaped, 16–36" (40–91 cm) long, bright green, smooth light green margin, flexible, pointed tip sometimes droops, 2–4 leaves per plant

Fruit: 3-parted elliptical green capsule, turning brown, 2" (5 cm) long

Bloom: summer

Cycle/Origin: perennial; native

Habitat: wet soils, open woods, meadows, freshwater and brackish marshes, along lakes, sun to partial shade

Range: eastern half and scattered locations in the western counties of the Carolinas

Notes: Can form colorful dense masses when growing in rich soils. Water loving, Virginia Iris is most common near the coast. Often planted near garden ponds, this fragrant and hardy flower is easily cultivated. Used medicinally by Cherokee Indians, but the roots are poisonous without proper preparation. Some people develop a rash after touching the foliage.

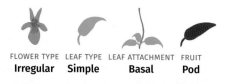

FLOWER TYPE
Irregular

LEAF TYPE
Simple

LEAF ATTACHMENT
Basal

FRUIT
Pod

Eastern Bluestar
Amsonia tabernaemontana

Family: Dogbane (Apocynaceae)

Height: 12–36" (30–91 cm)

Flower: loose round cluster, 3–6" (7.5–15 cm) wide, of a few to many blue-to-lavender flowers; each star-shaped flower, 1" (2.5 cm) wide, composed of 5 narrow petals fused into a slender tube and flaring out

Leaf: broadly lance-shaped, 3–6" (7.5–15 cm) long, bright green, turning golden yellow in fall, prominent whitish middle vein above, fine hairs below

Fruit: cylindrical greenish pod, turning brown, 3–5" (7.5–13 cm) long; pods are erect and found in pairs

Bloom: late spring

Cycle/Origin: perennial; native

Habitat: moist sandy soils, open woods, roadsides, sun

Range: throughout

Notes: Often cultivated in wildlife or perennial gardens or planted in masses for borders. Wonderful floral resource that attracts butterflies, bees and hummingbirds. Closely related to milkweed, the stem exudes a milky sap when broken. The sap does not seem to contain the deadly alkaloids of milkweed, but it does discourage browsing by deer—a boon for gardeners. The leaf shape of Eastern Bluestar is somewhat variable, as there are three recognized varieties of this species.

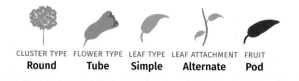

CLUSTER TYPE	FLOWER TYPE	LEAF TYPE	LEAF ATTACHMENT	FRUIT
Round	**Tube**	**Simple**	**Alternate**	**Pod**

Wild Lupine
Lupinus perennis

Family: Pea or Bean (Fabaceae)

Height: 12–36" (30–91 cm)

Flower: spike cluster, 3–7" (7.5–18 cm) long, of pea-like blue, pink or white flowers; individual flower, ⅔" (1.6 cm) wide, is made up of what appears to be 3 petals (called, from the top down, standard, wing and keel), but are actually 5 petals fused together

Leaf: palmate, 5–10" (13–25 cm) wide, made up of 7–11 small leaflets; leafstalk basally attached

Fruit: fuzzy green fruit, turning black, up to 2" (5 cm) long, pea-pod-shaped, containing 10–20 small brown-to-black seeds

Bloom: late spring, early summer

Cycle/Origin: perennial; native

Habitat: dry sandy soils, open woods, fields, roadsides, sun

Range: eastern half of the Carolinas

Notes: Found in sand dunes, clearings and open woods in the eastern half of the Carolinas. These pea-like flowers open under the weight of an insect, revealing horned-shaped stamens that deposit pollen on the visitor. Range overlaps with the closely related Oak Ridge Lupine (*L. diffusus*) (not shown), and the particularly showy Lady Lupine (*L. villosus*). American Indians rubbed the leaves on their skin, as they believed a compound in it helped them control horses. A larval host for the rare frosted elfin butterfly.

CLUSTER TYPE	FLOWER TYPE	LEAF TYPE	LEAF ATTACHMENT	FRUIT
Spike	**Irregular**	**Palmate**	**Basal**	**Pod**

41

Pickerelweed
Pontederia cordata

Family: Pickerelweed (Pontederiaceae)

Height: aquatic

Flower: spike cluster, 4–6" (10–15 cm) long, of blue-to-violet flowers; individual flower, ½" (1 cm) long, is composed of 3 upper petals (the middle upper petal has 2 small yellow spots) and 3 lower petals

Leaf: heart- or lance-shaped, 4–10" (10–25 cm) long and ½–6" (1–15 cm) wide, waxy, parallel veins, smooth margin, indented at base where stalk attaches; basal leaves rise from an underwater root

Bloom: summer, fall

Cycle/Origin: perennial; native

Habitat: lakes, wetlands, ponds, streams, wet roadside ditches, freshwater marshes, full to partial sun

Range: throughout

Notes: Pickerelweed is an aquatic plant rooted to the bottoms of bodies of fresh water or wet areas. Its leaves and flowers protrude above the water. Forms large colonies, spreading by short rhizomes. Preferring shallow water, Pickerelweed helps filter polluted water in marshes. Common name refers to the Pickerel, a fish that shares a similar aquatic habitat. Pickerelweed is a good choice for a water garden. Geese and muskrats eat the leaves. Flowers are highly attractive to pollinating insects. Its young leaves are edible in salads, and the roasted or dried seeds are nutritious.

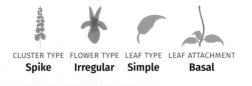

CLUSTER TYPE **Spike** FLOWER TYPE **Irregular** LEAF TYPE **Simple** LEAF ATTACHMENT **Basal**

Blue Mistflower

Conoclinium coelestinum

Family: Aster (Asteraceae)

Height: 12–36" (30–91 cm)

Flower: disk-shaped flat cluster, 4–8" (10–20 cm) wide, of lilac blue-to-magenta flower heads; each flower head made up of 40–70 tubular disk flowers that are cupped by pointed green bracts with burgundy tips

Leaf: arrowhead-shaped, 2–4" (5–10 cm) long, deeply grooved above and with a round-toothed margin; lower leaves smaller than upper leaves; oppositely attached to single fuzzy green or red stem

Bloom: summer, fall

Cycle/Origin: perennial; native

Habitat: moist soils, thickets, low woods, stream banks, roadside ditches, meadows, sun to partial shade

Range: eastern two-thirds of the Carolinas

Notes: Blue Mistflower is similar to plants in the genus *Ageratum* and is even commonly called Wild Ageratum. Frequently cultivated in butterfly and perennial gardens along with *Ageratum* plants, which are also in the Aster family. Produces eye-catching blooms when planted in masses in a garden. Attracts a multitude of butterflies, large and small, bees, and many other insect pollinators. The North Carolina Department of Transportation uses this species in highway plantings.

CLUSTER TYPE **Flat**   FLOWER TYPE **Composite**   LEAF TYPE **Simple**   LEAF ATTACHMENT **Opposite**

fruit

Bursting-Heart
Euonymus americanus

Family: Bittersweet (Celastraceae)

Height: 4–6' (1.2–1.8 m); shrub

Flower: purplish green or cream-colored, ½" (1 cm) wide, 5 petals circling a green center; single or groups of 2–3 inconspicuous flowers on stalks growing from leaf attachment (axis); many flowers per plant

Leaf: oval, 1½–4" (4–10 cm) long, pointed at both ends, finely toothed, attached to 4-angled twigs

Fruit: bright red capsule, ⅝" (1.5 cm) wide, rounded, warty, 3-lobed, splits open to reveal 4–5 fleshy orange-to-scarlet seeds

Bloom: summer

Cycle/Origin: perennial; native

Habitat: moist to dry sandy soils, rich deciduous woods, wooded slopes, streamsides, near springs, swamps, partial shade to full sun

Range: throughout

Notes: This open sprawling bush is notable not for its dull flowers, but for its bright red fruit and yellow, orange and red fall leaves. Also called American Strawberry Bush due to the unopened fruit, which resemble strawberries. All parts of this plant are said to be poisonous, but wild turkeys and songbirds eat the seeds without apparent ill effects. Usually deciduous (sometimes evergreen), the green foliage is a favorite food of deer and rabbits.

FLOWER TYPE	LEAF TYPE	LEAF ATTACHMENT	FRUIT
Regular	**Simple**	**Opposite**	**Pod**

fruit

Smooth Solomon's Seal
Polygonatum biflorum

Family: Asparagus (Asparagaceae)

Height: 1–4' (30–122 cm)

Flower: green, ½–1" (1–2.5 cm) long, bell-shaped, 6 petals; flowers hang in groups of 2–10 (mostly 2) on stalks, 1" (2.5 cm) long, which arise from leaf attachment

Leaf: lance-shaped, 2–6" (5–15 cm) long, toothless, stalkless, clasps upper part of arching stem; conspicuous parallel veining makes the leaf look light green

Fruit: round green berry, turning blue to black, ¼" (.6 cm) wide; hanging in clusters of 2–10 (usually 2) berries

Bloom: spring

Cycle/Origin: perennial; native

Habitat: moist soils, deciduous woods, thickets, shade

Range: most of the Carolinas

Notes: Also called True Solomon's Seal, use this rhyme to distinguish between this species and False Solomon's Seal: "Solomon's Seal, to be real, must have flowers along its keel." Distinguished by long arching stems that grow up to 6½ feet (2 m) tall. When a stalk breaks away, it leaves a distinctive round mark resembling the seal of King Solomon. Species name suggests two flowers, but it can grow up to ten per leaf axis. Grows from a large underground stem, which American Indians gathered for food. However, the stems may leave one's mouth tingling or numb.

FLOWER TYPE
Bell

LEAF TYPE
Simple

LEAF ATTACHMENT
Alternate

FRUIT
Berry

Waterspider Bog Orchid
Habenaria repens

Family: Orchid (Orchidaceae)

Height: 4–36" (10–91 cm); semi-aquatic

Flower: dense spike cluster, 1–3" (2.5–7.5 cm) long, of numerous greenish white flowers; each flower, ¾" (2 cm) wide, thin side petals curve upward and outward; shape of flower resembles a small spider; cluster appears overall yellowish green

Leaf: lance-shaped, 2–9" (5–23 cm) long, succulent, edges curl inward; leaves alternately clasping stem, getting progressively smaller toward top of stem

Fruit: thin reddish brown capsule, ⅓–⅝" (.8–1.5 cm) long

Bloom: spring, summer, fall

Cycle/Origin: perennial; native

Habitat: wet soils, bogs, marshes, wet places on land such as roadside ditches, lakeshores, edges of ponds or stream margins, sun

Range: southeastern North Carolina; eastern half of South Carolina

Notes: "Bog Orchid" is a good name for this semi-aquatic flower. Almost flat when floating in shallow water, but erect in wet earth. Common, but hard to spot since it often grows among floating mats of other aquatic vegetation, blending in with the leaves. Spreads by runners and plantlets, sometimes forming large colonies. *Repens* is Latin for "creeping," referring to its growing habit. Flowers emit a strong odor at night, probably to attract moths.

CLUSTER TYPE	FLOWER TYPE	LEAF TYPE	LEAF ATTACHMENT	LEAF ATTACHMENT	FRUIT
Spike	**Regular**	**Simple**	**Alternate**	**Clasping**	**Pod**

fruit

Jack-in-the-pulpit

Arisaema triphyllum

Family: Arum (Araceae)

Height: 12–36" (30–91 cm)

Flower: erect spike cluster, 2–3" (5–7.5 cm) long, of a green "club" (spadix or "Jack") sitting inside a green striped or mottled purplish "hood" (spathe or "pulpit") at top of a single stalk; spadix base is lined with tiny male or female flowers, protected by the spathe

Leaf: compound, 5–12" (13–30 cm) long, of 3 leaflets, dull green, smooth margin, deeply veined; 1–2 (female plant has 2; male has 1) leaves per plant

Fruit: shiny green berry, turning red in fall, ½" (1 cm) wide, found in cone-shaped clusters

Bloom: spring

Cycle/Origin: perennial; native

Habitat: wet soils, bogs, moist deciduous woods, shade

Range: throughout

Notes: Also called Indian Turnip because American Indians cooked its short, thickened, underground stem (corm) as food. However, no part of the plant is edible as it contains calcium oxalate crystals, which cause a burning sensation in the mouth. Its large three-parted leaves are often confused with those of White Trillium (pg. 293), but each leaflet of Jack-in-the-pulpit has a deep vein around its margin. If disturbed or affected by other stress, the female plant declines in vigor and may stop producing fruit.

CLUSTER TYPE
Spike

LEAF TYPE
Compound

LEAF ATTACHMENT
Alternate

FRUIT
Berry

Crane Fly Orchid
Tipularia discolor

Family: Orchid (Orchidaceae)

Height: 8–20" (20–50 cm)

Flower: very loose spike cluster, 4–8" (10–20 cm) long, of many green and maroon-brown flowers; each flower, ½" (1 cm) wide, 3 pointed sepals, 3 petals; central petal skewed from rest, forming a lighter-colored lip and thin translucent green spur; green center column is blunted and cylindrical

Leaf: oval, 2–4" (5–10 cm) long, dull green with raised maroon spots above, shiny beet red below, wavy margin, on a long leafstalk; 1 leaf per plant

Fruit: pointed oval green pod, turning reddish brown, ½" (1 cm) long, drooping

Bloom: summer

Cycle/Origin: perennial; native

Habitat: rich soils, oak-pine woods, under sweetgum trees

Range: throughout

Notes: The single leaf emerges in fall, persists through winter and spring and wilts before the plant flowers in summer. Flower resembles a small crane fly, thus the common name. In western North Carolina, may be mistaken for Adam and Eve (*Aplectrum hyemale*) (not shown), which has a striped, green-and-white leaf and pinkish purple-and-cream flowers. Pollinated by small moths. Oddly, pollen attaches to and is transported on one of the moth's compound eyes.

CLUSTER TYPE **Spike** FLOWER TYPE **Regular** LEAF TYPE **Simple** LEAF ATTACHMENT **Basal** FRUIT **Pod**

Orange Milkwort
Polygala lutea

Family: Milkwort (Polygalaceae)

Height: 6–15" (15–38 cm)

Flower: dense spike (can be round) cluster, ½–1½" (1–4 cm) long, of many tiny bright orange flowers with sharply pointed tips; each flower made up of 3 fused petals and 5 sepals, pointed "wings" formed by 2 of the sepals; leafless flower stalk

Leaf: basal, oval, 1–2" (2.5–5 cm) long; stem leaf, lance-shaped, ⅝–1" (1.5–2.5 cm) long; leaves narrower farther up stem; both types wider toward tip, fleshy

Bloom: spring, summer, fall

Cycle/Origin: biennial; native

Habitat: sandy or acid soils, swamps, bogs, open pinewoods, cypress pond edges, ditches, sun to partial shade

Range: eastern half of the Carolinas

Notes: Low growing, often among taller grasses, but conspicuous due to its orange flower clusters. Appears like a single flower; actually is a cluster of numerous and densely packed, tiny flowers. Also called Candyflower or Bog Bachelor's Button. *Polygala* means "much milk," for the belief that cows eating plants in the genus would produce more milk. *Lutea* is Latin for "yellow," the color of the cluster when dried. American Indians used the plant to treat heart and blood diseases.

CLUSTER TYPE	FLOWER TYPE	LEAF TYPE	LEAF ATTACHMENT	LEAF ATTACHMENT
Spike	**Irregular**	**Simple**	**Alternate**	**Basal**

fruit

Jewelweed

Impatiens capensis

Family: Touch-me-not (Balsaminaceae)

Height: 3–5' (.9–1.5 m)

Flower: orange, 1" (2.5 cm) long, covered with reddish brown spots, has a large open mouth that leads to a long thin sharp-curved tube (spur)

Leaf: oval, 1–3" (2.5–7.5 cm) long, sharp-toothed margin, on short leafstalk, 1" (2.5 cm) long

Fruit: thin pod-like green container, 1¼" (3 cm) long, banana-shaped, contains small brown seeds

Bloom: summer, fall

Cycle/Origin: annual; native

Habitat: wet soils, wetlands, along streams, bogs, bottomlands, moist forests, shade

Range: throughout

Notes: When ripe, the pod-like containers explode when touched, dispersing seeds in all directions. This action, along with the dark spots on its flowers, give rise to its other common name of Spotted-Touch-me-not. Stems are nearly translucent and contain a slimy sap that can be used to soothe the sting from nettles or Poison Ivy. Scraping off the dark brown covering of a ripe seed reveals a sky blue nutlet inside. An important nectar source for hummingbirds. Pale Touch-me-not (*I. pallida*) (not shown) of the North Carolina mountains is similar, but has yellow flowers that have fewer spots than this species.

FLOWER TYPE	LEAF TYPE	LEAF ATTACHMENT	FRUIT
Tube	**Simple**	**Alternate**	**Pod**

fruit

Crossvine
Bignonia capreolata

Family: Trumpet Creeper (Bignoniaceae)

Height: 40–56' (12.2–17 m); vine

Flower: orange and yellow, 1½–2" (4–5 cm) long, trumpet-shaped, made up of 5 fused petals, orange outside, yellow with orange streaks inside the throat; many hanging flowers per vine

Leaf: compound, 2 oval leaflets, 2½–6" (6–15 cm) long, smooth margins, pointed tips; 1 branching tendril with sticky cups on ends, semi-evergreen, turning reddish purple; square dark purple stem

Fruit: J-shaped greenish pod, turning reddish brown, 6" (15 cm) long, flat and thin; has many seeds

Bloom: spring, summer

Cycle/Origin: perennial; native

Habitat: fertile woods, floodplains, swamps, roadsides, sun

Range: throughout

Notes: Named for the cross shape seen in the interior of its cut stem. Produces masses of beautiful, showy flowers when in full sun. Modified leaflet tendrils have sticky cups that enable it to cling to a building or tree to reach sunlight; it will also drape over a wall or fence. Can be used to replace non-native clinging vines on trellises or arbors, but it is aggressive and must be trimmed back regularly or it will invade areas where it is not wanted. Often planted in wildlife gardens, as its abundant nectar attracts hummingbirds.

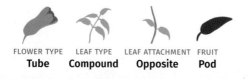

FLOWER TYPE	LEAF TYPE	LEAF ATTACHMENT	FRUIT
Tube	**Compound**	**Opposite**	**Pod**

fruit

Butterfly-weed
Asclepias tuberosa

Family: Dogbane (Apocynaceae)

Height: 12–24" (30–61 cm)

Flower: large flat cluster, 2–3" (5–7.5 cm) wide, of small, deep orange flowers; each flower, ⅜" (.9 cm) wide, of downward-curving petals; flower color varies from all yellow to red

Leaf: lance-shaped, 2–6" (5–15 cm) long, widens near tip, hairy, smooth margin; mostly alternately (sometimes oppositely) attached near top of hairy stem

Fruit: erect narrow green pod, turning brown, 6" (15 cm) long, covered with fine hairs; small clusters of pods have large brown seeds with silken "parachutes" to carry away each seed

Bloom: summer

Cycle/Origin: perennial; native

Habitat: dry (prefers sandy) soils, pastures, along roads, sun

Range: throughout

Notes: Also called Butterfly Milkweed. Found in clumps, this true milkweed lacks milky sap; instead, its stem and leaves contain clear sap. Species name *tuberosa* refers to its large taproot, which makes it nearly impossible to transplant. Can be grown from seed. Single stems branch only near the top and flower clusters harbor up to 25 individual flowers. Roots and stems have been used in folk medicine. A host for Queen and Monarch butterfly caterpillars.

CLUSTER TYPE	FLOWER TYPE	LEAF TYPE	LEAF ATTACHMENT	FRUIT
Flat	**Irregular**	**Simple**	**Alternate**	**Pod**

Indian Blanket

Gaillardia pulchella

Family: Aster (Asteraceae)

Height: 2–24" (5–61 cm)

Flower: daisy-like, tricolored flower head, 2–3" (5–7.5 cm) wide, made up of 8–14 triangular (orange, red or purple) petals with 3-lobed (usually yellow or orange) tips surrounding a domed maroon center

Leaf: narrowly oblong or spoon-shaped, ½–3½" (1–9 cm) long, fuzzy above, usually a smooth (sometimes toothed or lobed) margin; upper leaves smaller and clasping; multi-branched, sticky-haired stem

Bloom: spring, summer, fall

Cycle/Origin: annual, perennial, biennial; native

Habitat: sand flats, dunes, old pastures, disturbed sites, sun

Range: scattered locations in the Carolinas, mostly along the coast

Notes: Also called Firewheel because the flower resembles a child's pinwheel, with its maroon center surrounded by an orange or red ring that, in turn, is encircled by a ring of yellow. Readily self-seeds and forms large colorful masses of flowers that blanket the ground, thus the common name, Indian Blanket. Many state highway departments plant this eye-catching flower along roads. Hardy and drought tolerant, it is often grown in wildflower gardens since it needs little care and the flowers last a long time. The flowers are a favorite of bees.

FLOWER TYPE LEAF TYPE LEAF ATTACHMENT
Composite **Simple** **Alternate**

Turk's-cap Lily
Lilium superbum

Family: Lily (Liliaceae)

Height: 3–10' (.9–3 m)

Flower: orange and yellow, 2–3" (5–7.5 cm) wide, 6 backward-curving petals (actually 3 petals and 3 sepals) circling central green star with yellow center; all petals covered with dark purplish spots

Leaf: narrowly lance-shaped, 2–10" (5–25 cm) long, sharply pointed tip; whorl of 4–20 leaves

Fruit: oblong angular green pod, turning brown when mature, 2" (5 cm) long

Bloom: summer

Cycle/Origin: perennial; native

Habitat: wet soils, meadows, woods, backwater swamps

Range: western mountainous counties of North Carolina

Notes: The tallest lily in eastern North America. Commonly found in streamside forests of Appalachian Mountain valleys and in impressive masses along the Blue Ridge Parkway. Once common along country roads, but occurs less often since ditches are now drained and mowed. Closely resembles Carolina Lily (pg. 71), but lacks that flower's sweet fragrance. Produces 3–30 showy, dangling flowers per plant. The curled-back flower petals look like a Turkish cap, hence part of the common name. Grows from a large scaly underground bulb, which American Indians gathered for food.

FLOWER TYPE
Regular

LEAF TYPE
Simple

LEAF ATTACHMENT
Whorl

FRUIT
Pod

Yellow Fringed Orchid
Platanthera ciliaris

Family: Orchid (Orchidaceae)

Height: 12–36" (30–91 cm)

Flower: cone-shaped loose spike cluster, 2–8" (5–20 cm) long, of 25–115 apricot-to-orange (sometimes yellow) flowers; each flower, 2" (5 cm) long, 3 petals form erect "hood," 2 form drooping side "wings," 1 tongue-like petal (lip) heavily fringed on edges with downward- and backward-curving spur

Leaf: lance-shaped, 2–16" (5–40 cm) long, pointed tip; leaves smaller toward top of smooth stem

Bloom: summer

Cycle/Origin: perennial; native

Habitat: acid seeps, pinewoods, stream or pond edges, marshes, roadsides, meadows, along railroads

Range: throughout

Notes: One of the showier wildflowers in the Carolinas in July and August, this species occurs in more kinds of habitats than do other orchids. A shorter relative, Crested Yellow Orchid (*P. cristata*) (not shown), has flowers that start blooming in June and have much shorter spurs. Although "Yellow" in the common name, the usually orange-colored flowers are pollinated by butterflies. Once common, and while apparently not at risk in the Carolinas, it is listed as threatened or endangered throughout most of its range. Thus, please do not dig up this plant or pick the flowers.

CLUSTER TYPE	FLOWER TYPE	LEAF TYPE	LEAF ATTACHMENT	LEAF ATTACHMENT
Spike	**Irregular**	**Simple**	**Alternate**	**Clasping**

Carolina Lily
Lilium michauxii

Family: Lily (Liliaceae)

Height: 1–4' (30–122 cm)

Flower: yellowish orange, 3" (7.5 cm) wide, 6 sharply backward-curving pointed petals (actually 3 petals and 3 sepals) around protruding dangling flower parts; each petal burnt orange on outer portion, becoming light orange, then green at base; petals covered with small maroon spots; 1–6 hanging flowers per stalk

Leaf: teardrop-shaped, 1½–4½" (4–11 cm) long, widest above the middle, fleshy, pointed tip, wavy edges; whorl of 3–10 leaves; 2–4 whorls per stem

Fruit: winged oval green pod, 1–2" (2.5–5 cm) long

Bloom: summer

Cycle/Origin: perennial; native

Habitat: moist soils, upland pine-oak forests, swamps, along roads, rich open woods, sun

Range: eastern third of the Carolinas

Notes: Carolina Lily became the official state *wildflower* of North Carolina in 2003. Should not to be confused with the state's official *flower*, American Dogwood, which is actually an early spring-blooming tree. The only native lily in the Carolinas with a sweet strong fragrance. Pollinated by butterflies such as Eastern Tiger Swallowtails. Similar to Turk's-cap Lily (pg. 67), but lacks the central green star, and its leaves are mostly along the middle of the stem.

FLOWER TYPE
Regular

LEAF TYPE
Simple

LEAF ATTACHMENT
Whorl

FRUIT
Pod

Pine Lily
Lilium catesbaei

Family: Lily (Liliaceae)

Height: 12–36" (30–91 cm)

Flower: orange or crimson, 3–4½" (7.5–11 cm) wide, spreading bowl-shaped, each of 6 petals curving outward and downward is broad, pointed, wavy-edged, has yellow base with magenta spots and on a green stalk that attaches at base of tall yellow-orange flower parts; 1–3 (usually 1) erect flowers at end of stalk

Leaf: flattened, grass-like, 1–3" (2.5–10 cm) long, pointed tip, grows upward or closely pressed to stem

Fruit: ridged oblong green capsule, 1–2" (2.5–5 cm) long

Bloom: summer, fall

Cycle/Origin: perennial; native

Habitat: moist soils, roadsides, sandhills, pitcher plant bogs, native Longleaf Pine and Slash Pine savannahs

Range: eastern half of the Carolinas

Notes: The largest flower of any native lily in North America. Needs sunlight provided by an open canopy, historically created by frequent fires in the wild. Once common, but now less so due to same-age pine plantations replacing native pine stands. Very difficult to find for purchase, but please don't dig up the plant or collect the seeds. Plant in moist spots in gardens to attract its main pollinators, the beautiful Palamedes and Spicebush Swallowtail butterflies.

FLOWER TYPE	LEAF TYPE	LEAF ATTACHMENT	FRUIT
Regular	**Simple**	**Alternate**	**Pod**

73

Deptford Pink
Dianthus armeria

Family: Pink (Caryophyllaceae)

Height: 6–24" (15–61 cm)

Flower: pink to rose, ½" (1 cm) wide, with 5 petals covered with tiny white spots, irregularly toothed edges; groups of 3–9 flowers; several groups per plant

Leaf: basal, narrow and grass-like, 1–4" (2.5–10 cm) long, light green, numerous, often covered with tiny white hairs; stem leaves (cauline), 5–10 pair, oppositely attached to hollow hairy stem

Bloom: spring, summer

Cycle/Origin: annual, biennial; non-native

Habitat: dry soils, old fields, open woods, roadsides, along railroads, disturbed areas, sun

Range: western two-thirds of North Carolina, northern one-third of South Carolina

Notes: Now naturalized throughout much of the Carolinas, this non-native wildflower was introduced from England. The first part of the common name refers to the town of Deptford (now part of London), where the species was apparently originally found. The genus *Dianthus* includes nearly 300 species, most of which are annuals originating from Europe. Closely related to carnations. The flowers are covered with white spots and have unusual jagged edges. Long needle-like bracts rise from the base of the flowers, extending beyond the petals.

FLOWER TYPE	LEAF TYPE	LEAF ATTACHMENT	LEAF ATTACHMENT
Regular	**Simple**	**Opposite**	**Basal**

Virginia Springbeauty
Claytonia virginica

Family: Miner's Lettuce (Montiaceae)

Height: 6–10" (15–25 cm)

Flower: white to pink to lavender, ½–¾" (1–2 cm) wide, 5 pink-veined petals and a slightly yellow-tinted center; flowers are showy and upright

Leaf: narrow and grass-like, 2–4" (5–10 cm) long; leaves oppositely attached midway up the stem; usually 1 to several pairs of leaves per plant

Bloom: early spring

Cycle/Origin: perennial; native

Habitat: wet soils, deciduous woods, clearings in woods

Range: throughout

Notes: An attractive flower that blooms early in spring, hence its common name. The pink veins on the petals act as runways to guide insects to the nectar. As they "taxi in," the insects load up on pollen by brushing against stamens, then fly to another flower, where they deposit a few grains onto the receptive stigma. Often grows in large patches, reproducing from small underground tubers. The potato-like tubers were once gathered for food, and as a result, Springbeauty populations are now reduced. Do not dig up this plant—a variety can be purchased at local garden centers. One of many plants in the Miner's Lettuce family, a group of about 500 species of plants worldwide.

FLOWER TYPE
Regular

LEAF TYPE
Simple

LEAF ATTACHMENT
Opposite

fruit

Pink Fuzzybean
Strophostyles umbellata

Family: Pea or Bean (Fabaceae)

Height: 2–7' (.6–2.1 m); vine

Flower: pink to lavender, ½–¾" (1–2 cm) wide, broadly pea-like; 3–4 flowers well above leaves on flower stalk, 12" (30 cm) long

Leaf: compound, 1¼–3¼" (3–8 cm) long, divided into 3 narrowly oval leaflets; each leaflet, ¾–2" (2–5 cm) long, smooth margin, blunt or pointed tip, hairy; leaves alternately attached to twining stem

Fruit: narrow green pod, turning dark brown, 1¼–2¼" (3–5.5 cm) long, shaped like a string bean and finely haired, contains many seeds

Bloom: summer, fall

Cycle/Origin: perennial; native

Habitat: dry rocky or sandy soils, woods, fields, disturbed sites, partial shade to sun

Range: throughout

Notes: Common name is for the pink flower and the hairy bean-like pod. Also called Wild Bean, it is often cultivated for its delicate flowers and its ability to quickly cover a trellis or fence. The annual Amberique-bean (*S. helvola*) (not shown) looks similar, but it has leaflets with two or three lobes. Bobwhite Quail, turkeys and doves enjoy the seeds of both of these members of the Pea or Bean family.

| FLOWER TYPE | LEAF TYPE | LEAF ATTACHMENT | FRUIT |
| Irregular | Compound | Alternate | Pod |

Pennsylvania Smartweed
Persicaria pensylvanica

Family: Buckwheat (Polygonaceae)

Height: 2–7' (.6–2.1 m)

Flower: cylindrical spike cluster, ⅝–2" (1.5–5 cm) long, of numerous pink (can be whitish pink or white) flowers; each tiny bowl-shaped flower made up of 5 bluntly fingernail-shaped petals and petal-like sepals around a white center

Leaf: lance-shaped, 5–6" (13–15 cm) long, slightly drooping, tip pointed, leafstalk encased with a smooth sheath; alternately attached to reddish nodes of stem; sticky-haired stem branches widely near base

Bloom: summer, fall

Cycle/Origin: annual; native

Habitat: moist to wet soils, freshwater or brackish mud flats, disturbed sites, waste ground, along railroads, sun

Range: throughout

Notes: "Smart" in the common name refers to the sharp burning sensation the leaves produce when eaten. The seeds are an outstanding food source for a wide variety of wildlife such as waterfowl, game birds, mice, raccoons, muskrats and fox squirrels. Plant in wildlife gardens to attract these interesting birds and animals. Pennsylvania Smartweed is one of many other species in the Buckwheat family in the Carolinas, with most considered somewhat weedy.

CLUSTER TYPE	FLOWER TYPE	LEAF TYPE	LEAF ATTACHMENT
Spike	**Regular**	**Simple**	**Alternate**

Littleleaf Sensitive-briar
Mimosa microphylla

Family: Pea or Bean (Fabaceae)

Height: 3–7' (.9–2.1 m); vine

Flower: round cluster, ¾" (2 cm) wide, of a multitude of tiny tubular bright pink flowers; flower parts supporting pollen rise above tubules, appearing like yellow dots floating in the air; each cluster grows singly on stalk

Leaf: twice compound, 2½–6" (6–15 cm) long, divided into 3–5 pair of oblong leaflets and again into 8–11 pair of tiny subleaflets; leaf on long thorny leafstalk attached to sprawling vine; thorns on stems shaped like a cat's claw

Fruit: long slim green pod, turning brown, 1½–3" (4–7.5 cm) long, sharp edges densely covered with thorns

Bloom: summer, fall

Cycle/Origin: perennial; native

Habitat: disturbed areas, edges of woods, fields, knolls, sun

Range: throughout

Notes: "Littleleaf" is for the tiny subleaflets, which are less than ¼ inch (.6 cm) long, and "Sensitive" is for their response to touch—they fold together for 4–5 minutes after being lightly touched. All subleaflets close even when only one nearby is tapped. This protects the foliage, presenting thorns on the leafstalks to any grazing deer or rabbits. Plant behavior usually doesn't occur quickly enough for us to detect the motion, but one is able to do so with this plant.

CLUSTER TYPE
Round

FLOWER TYPE
Tube

LEAF TYPE
Twice Compound

LEAF ATTACHMENT
Alternate

FRUIT
Pod

Procession Flower
Polygala incarnata

Family: Milkwort (Polygalaceae)

Height: 8–24" (20–61 cm)

Flower: short spike cluster, ½–1½" (1–4 cm) long, of densely clustered bright pink-to-pale lavender flowers; each slim flower, ½" (1 cm) long, petals forming tube, spreading into 8 short pointed lobes; white center; pointed, purplish white or greenish white bracts

Leaf: narrowly oblong, ¼–½" (.6–1 cm) long, pointed tip; leaves close against and sparse along slender smooth stem; stem single or with a few branches

Fruit: oval, flattened, purplish green pod; blunted on each end; contains black seeds

Bloom: summer

Cycle/Origin: annual; native

Habitat: dry or sandy soils, forest edges, woods, fields, sun

Range: throughout most of the Carolinas

Notes: Named Procession Flower for its historical use in garlands worn or carried by Catholics celebrating The Fifth Sunday After Easter. Has the largest individual flower of any of the tiny-flowered milkworts in the Carolinas, but looks like a single short colorful flower atop an apparently leafless stem from a distance. Flowers open a few at a time, from the bottom up. The root was used for respiratory ailments and is still sold in some pharmacies. Apparently not at risk in the Carolinas, but imperiled in much of the Midwest.

CLUSTER TYPE
Spike

FLOWER TYPE
Irregular

LEAF TYPE
Simple

LEAF ATTACHMENT
Alternate

FRUIT
Pod

Snakemouth Orchid

Pogonia ophioglossoides

Family: Orchid (Orchidaceae)

Height: 8–16" (20–40 cm)

Flower: pale or rose pink (sometimes lavender or white), ½–1½" (1–4 cm) long, 3 slim elliptical sepals and 2 similar petals; tongue-like horizontal modified third petal, fringed on edges, veined with magenta and with a line of pink, white, then yellow bristles mid-point; bract beneath flower; 1–3 flowers atop stem

Leaf: lance-shaped, 1–3½" (2.5–9 cm) long, pointed tip, 1 cauline leaf clasps the stem midway, 1 leaf clasps the base

Bloom: summer

Cycle/Origin: perennial; native

Habitat: wet or acid soils, bogs, roadsides, open meadows, along railroads, abandoned gravel pits, sun

Range: scattered throughout

Notes: Greek for "bearded," the genus name *Pogonia* refers to the hair-like bristles midline on the lower petal. Pollen-seeking bees are fooled by the yellow bristles—the real pollen is actually hidden and deposited on the back of the unsuspecting bee, to be carried away to the next flower. Although uncommon in the Carolinas, it can be abundant where it does occur, forming large colonies by spreading runners.

FLOWER TYPE
Irregular

LEAF TYPE
Simple

LEAF ATTACHMENT
Basal

LEAF ATTACHMENT
Clasping

Sandywoods Chaffhead

Carphephorus bellidifolius

Family: Aster (Asteraceae)

Height: 8–36" (20–91 cm)

Flower: loose flat cluster, 1–1½" (2.5–4 cm) wide, of 2–40 pink-to-lavender flower heads; each flower head, ¼" (.6 cm) wide, made up of tubular disk flowers with conspicuous protruding flower parts

Leaf: numerous basal, spoon-shaped, 1½–6" (4–15 cm) long, stalked; stem (cauline) leaf, narrow, lance-shaped, becoming much smaller farther up the stem, stalkless; cauline leaves alternate at wide intervals along the several smooth stems

Bloom: summer, fall

Cycle/Origin: perennial; native

Habitat: dry sandy soils, sandhills, roadsides, scrub oak woodlands, pine barrens, partial to full sun

Range: eastern half of the Carolinas

Notes: When present, this aster is an indicator that you are in the Carolina pinelands. Most common in the sandhills and along the Carolina coast, it tolerates even drier soils than do others in the genus. Sandywoods Chaffhead is affectionately regarded by butterfly watchers since its flowers are an excellent nectar source for a variety of butterflies, which visit the blooms along country roads.

CLUSTER TYPE	FLOWER TYPE	LEAF TYPE	LEAF ATTACHMENT	LEAF ATTACHMENT
Flat	**Composite**	**Simple**	**Alternate**	**Basal**

Trailing Phlox
Phlox nivalis

Family: Phlox (Polemoniaceae)

Height: 1–12" (2.5–30 cm)

Flower: pink or pale lavender to white, 1" (2.5 cm) wide, made up of 5 jagged- or smooth-tipped, heart-shaped petals surrounding a star-shaped center with a pink dot near the points of the star; petals fused to form a long narrow tube; 2–3 flowers sit atop erect reddish stalk that is hairy and sticky

Leaf: narrow, awl-shaped, ½–1" (1–2.5 cm) long; shiny evergreen leaves densely packed and oppositely attached along a woody hairy stem; stem spreads along the ground

Bloom: spring

Cycle/Origin: perennial; native

Habitat: dry sandy soils, acid soils, slopes, deciduous woods, pinewoods, roadsides, sun to partial shade

Range: western two-thirds of South Carolina, middle third of North Carolina

Notes: Trailing Phlox is found in large colorful patches due to its creeping stems, hence "Trailing" in its common name. The genus name *Phlox* is Greek for "flame" and refers to the twisted shape of the closed flower bud. Look for the heart-shaped petals with a shallow notch at the top of the heart to help identify this flower.

FLOWER TYPE
Regular

LEAF TYPE
Simple

LEAF ATTACHMENT
Opposite

Annual Phlox
Phlox drummondii

Family: Phlox (Polemoniaceae)

Height: 4–24" (10–61 cm)

Flower: dark pink (usually), but variable, 1" (2.5 cm) wide, made of 5 blunt-tipped overlapping petals surrounding contrasting center, petals fuse at base to form a long narrow tube; loosely clustered flowers sit high above leaves atop hairy sticky stem

Leaf: oblong, 2–4" (5–10 cm) long; lower leaves oppositely attached, upper leaves alternate on stem that has many glandular hairs

Bloom: spring, summer

Cycle/Origin: annual; native

Habitat: dry to moist sandy soils, roadsides, disturbed areas, old fields, abandoned lawns, dunes, sun

Range: eastern half of the Carolinas

Notes: Native to central and eastern Texas, Annual Phlox is widely cultivated and has escaped and naturalized in the sandy soils of disturbed areas in the eastern half of the Carolinas. The flowers come in a variety of colors, including pink, magenta, lavender, red and white. This is a fragrant flower that likes cool spring weather and does best at temperatures below 85°F (29°C). Annual phlox is widely planted or naturalized along roadsides.

FLOWER TYPE **Regular**   LEAF TYPE **Simple**   LEAF ATTACHMENT **Alternate**   LEAF ATTACHMENT **Opposite**

fruit

Handsome Harry
Rhexia virginica

Family: Meadowbeauty (Melastomataceae)

Height: 8–36" (20–91 cm)

Flower: bright pink or lavender, 1–1½" (2.5–4 cm) wide, 4 hairy irregular oval or heart-shaped petals; curved, dangling, yellow flower parts; urn-shaped calyx

Leaf: oval, 1–3" (2.5–7.5 cm) long, green or with red patches, hairy, fine-toothed margin; each pair of leaves rotated at right angles to next pair

Fruit: pitcher-shaped green pod, turning bright red to brown, ⅔" (1.6 cm) long, 4-sided with triangular point at each corner, hole opens at top when ripe

Bloom: summer, fall

Cycle/Origin: perennial; native

Habitat: moist soils, roadsides, pond edges, pinewoods, bogs

Range: throughout the Carolinas, except in the central counties of each state

Notes: Of the seven species of meadowbeauty in the Carolinas, this is the most widespread, occurring throughout the eastern half of the U.S. Mostly pollinated by bumblebees by "buzz pollination." The bee vibrates its flying muscles after landing, causing pollen to flow out of the anthers. Collecting the pollen to eat later, the bee unwittingly pollinates the next flower upon landing. The flowers close upon pollination, but will remain open for two days if not pollinated, with the yellow stamens turning red on the second day.

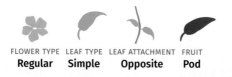

FLOWER TYPE **Regular**　　LEAF TYPE **Simple**　　LEAF ATTACHMENT **Opposite**　　FRUIT **Pod**

fruit

Maryland Meadowbeauty

Rhexia mariana

Family: Meadowbeauty (Melastomataceae)

Height: 8–36" (20–91 cm)

Flower: pale pink (can be lavender or white barely washed with pink), 1–2" (2.5–5 cm) wide, 4 irregular oval petals; long, curved, dangling, orange flower parts; pitcher-shaped green or red calyx

Leaf: lance-shaped, 1–2" (2.5–5 cm) long, green with red spots, hairy above and below, toothed red or green margin with red hair projecting from each tooth; squarish stem has short to very long white hairs

Fruit: vase-shaped red pod, ¼" (.6 cm) long, 4-sided

Bloom: summer, fall

Cycle/Origin: perennial; native

Habitat: moist soils, marshes, ditches, along railroads, pond edges, wet meadows, along streams, sun

Range: throughout

Notes: The four pair of prominent anthers projecting from a pitcher-shaped calyx and the vase-shaped seedpods lead to another common name, Meadow Pitcher. Has white hairs on stem, with the white-flowered variety tending to have the longest hairs. This particular species spreads by creeping underground stems to form large colonies. Planted in wet spots in gardens, it makes a good ground cover with long-blooming flowers. Young leaves of plants in the genus *Rhexia* have a tart, sweet taste and can be eaten raw in salads.

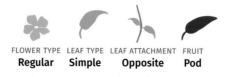

FLOWER TYPE
Regular

LEAF TYPE
Simple

LEAF ATTACHMENT
Opposite

FRUIT
Pod

Spotted Beebalm
Monarda punctata

Family: Mint (Lamiaceae)

Height: 12–36" (30–91 cm)

Flower: ragged spike cluster, 1–2" (2.5–5 cm) wide, of lance-shaped, downward-curving, prominent pink-to-purple or white and green bracts (often mistaken for petals) and yellowish flowers with maroon spots; each flower, 1" (2.5 cm) long, of 2 petals (lips); 2–5 clusters alternate with bracts along upper stem

Leaf: lance-shaped, 1–3" (2.5–7.5 cm) long, oppositely attached to hairy square grayish stem

Bloom: summer, fall

Cycle/Origin: annual, perennial, biennial; native

Habitat: dry sandy soils, dunes, roadsides, rocky woodlands

Range: throughout North Carolina, eastern half of South Carolina

Notes: Plants in the Mint family can be identified by their square stems and oppositely attached leaves. In addition, the stems and leaves of most plants in the family are scented. Spotted Bee Balm has a unique tiered arrangement in its flowerheads that somewhat resembles a Chinese pagoda. Sometimes called Dotted Horsemint, American Indians used it to treat fevers and colds or hung it up to dry, perfuming a lodge with its minty fragrance. Naturally occurs most commonly in the flatlands and nearby hills close to the Carolina coast. Often cultivated in gardens, its nectar attracts hummingbirds.

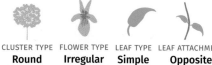

CLUSTER TYPE
Round

FLOWER TYPE
Irregular

LEAF TYPE
Simple

LEAF ATTACHMENT
Opposite

fruit

Perennial Pea
Lathyrus latifolius

Family: Pea or Bean (Fabaceae)

Height: 1–7' (.3–2.1 m); vine

Flower: loose spike cluster, 1–5" (2.5–13 cm) long, of 4–10 pea-like pink flowers; each flower, 1" (2.5 cm) wide, on a long stem

Leaf: compound, 4" (10 cm) long, of 2 lance-shaped or elliptical leaflets; each leaflet, 1–3" (2.5–7.5 cm) long, at end of a flat winged stalk; may have a forked thread-like projection (tendril) from the tip of leafstalk; multiple stems with many branches

Fruit: slender bean-like green pod, turning yellow, 2½–4" (6–10 cm) long, contains 10–15 cylindrical poisonous blackish seeds

Bloom: summer, fall

Cycle/Origin: perennial; non-native

Habitat: disturbed soils, roadsides, fields, waste areas, sun

Range: throughout

Notes: This non-native plant is very invasive, readily escaping from cultivation or overrunning a garden. A weak-stemmed vine that climbs on other plants by taking hold with its forked tendrils. Has two pair of narrow pointed appendages (stipules) at the base of each leafstalk. Stems and leafstalks are winged. However, the flower stalk lacks wings and can grow to up to 8 inches (20 cm) long. Flowers are usually pink, but can be pink and white or blue to white.

CLUSTER TYPE	FLOWER TYPE	LEAF TYPE	LEAF ATTACHMENT	FRUIT
Spike	**Irregular**	**Compound**	**Alternate**	**Pod**

Bashful Wakerobin

Trillium catesbaei

Family: Lily (Liliaceae)

Height: 8–20" (20–50 cm)

Flower: pink to white, turning rose-pink with age, 1½–2" (4–5 cm) long, of 3 wavy-edged, strongly backward-curling petals with dark rose veins and whitish bases, 3 bluntly pointed, purplish green sepals and long curved yellow flower parts; single large flower atop stalk droops below the leaves

Leaf: oval, 3–6" (7.5–15 cm) long, green or slightly purplish, pointed tip, slightly raised smooth margin; whorl of 3 leaves at top of purplish green stem

Fruit: oval green berry, turning white, ½" (1 cm) long

Bloom: spring, summer

Cycle/Origin: perennial; native

Habitat: moist rich acid soils, slopes, often near tree bases in bottomland forests, rhododendron thickets, shade

Range: western two-thirds of the Carolinas

Notes: "Bashful" is for the nodding flower, appearing to hide its blushing pink "face" below its leaves. The most abundant trillium in the Carolinas, especially common on the wide plateau between the flat eastern coast and the Appalachian Mountains in the western portion of each state. *Trillium* means "triple" in Latin, referring to the three petals and three sepals of the flower. Named for Mark Catesby, who published the first book about plants of the Carolinas in 1731.

FLOWER TYPE
Regular

LEAF TYPE
Simple

LEAF ATTACHMENT
Whorl

FRUIT
Berry

Virginia Tephrosia
Tephrosia virginiana

Family: Pea or Bean (Fabaceae)

Height: 12–24" (30–61 cm)

Flower: compact spike cluster, 1½–3" (4–7.5 cm) long, of pink-and-white pea-like flowers; each flower, ¾" (2 cm) long, of white or cream upper petal (standard), pink wings and lower rose pink petals (keel); hairy pointed bell-shaped sepals (calyx)

Leaf: compound, 7" (18 cm) long, feather-like, of 11–25 elliptical, bluntly pointed leaflets; each leaflet, 1" (2.5 cm) long, grayish, hairy, oppositely attached; leaves alternate on multiple stems with long hairs

Fruit: hairy green pod, turning brown to black, 2" (5 cm) long, pea-like, flattened lengthwise

Bloom: summer

Cycle/Origin: perennial; native

Habitat: dry sandy acid soils, thickets, woods, dunes, sun

Range: throughout

Notes: *Tephros* is Greek for "hoary," for the grayish cast produced by the hairs on the leaves and stems. Some wildlife and livestock avoid the poisonous leaves, thus another common name, Goat's Rue. Both Southern and Northern Cloudywing butterfly caterpillars utilize this plant for food, despite the leaves containing rotenone, a chemical used as an insecticide. American Indians put the leaves in streams to stun fish, scooping them up when they floated to the surface.

CLUSTER TYPE
Spike

FLOWER TYPE
Irregular

LEAF TYPE
Compound

LEAF ATTACHMENT
Alternate

FRUIT
Pod

fruit

Carolina Rose
Rosa carolina

Family: Rose (Rosaceae)

Height: 24–36" (61–91 cm); shrub

Flower: pink (sometimes white), 2" (5 cm) wide, made up of 5 thumbnail- or heart-shaped petals; broad center of more than 50 yellow flower parts (stamens)

Leaf: compound, composed of 5–7 broadly oval leaflets; each leaflet, ¾–1½" (2–4 cm) long, smooth, pointed tip, coarse-toothed margin; olive green or reddish stem with straight thorns; leaves turn dull red in fall

Fruit: globular green fruit, turning slightly yellow, then red, ¼" (.6 cm) wide, pulpy; hangs on the shrub until the next spring; referred to as a rose hip

Bloom: summer

Cycle/Origin: perennial; native

Habitat: dry soils, thickets, meadows, fencerows, sun

Range: throughout

Notes: Wild roses have petals in a single layer, while most cultivated roses have many layers of petals. Rose hips are edible and have seeds rich with vitamin C; they stay on the shrub in winter, providing food for wildlife. Sometimes called Pasture Rose, this species has fragrant flowers and spreads by suckers, forming thickets that make good cover for birds and other animals. The non-native Cherokee Rose *(R. laevigata)* (not shown), seen along country roads in southern South Carolina, has only 3 leaflets per leaf and long spines on its large rose hips.

FLOWER TYPE	LEAF TYPE	LEAF ATTACHMENT	FRUIT
Regular	**Compound**	**Alternate**	**Berry**

Pink Lady's Slipper
Cypripedium acaule

Family: Orchid (Orchidaceae)

Height: 6–15" (15–38 cm)

Flower: deep rosy pink, 2½" (6 cm) long, inflated lower petal (slipper) with red veins and a groove down the middle, 3 pointed, twisted, greenish brown sepals; 1 large flower tops each leafless stalk

Leaf: broadly elliptical, 4–10" (10–25 cm) long, silvery below, deep parallel veins; basally attached in pairs

Fruit: pod-like green container, turning brown, 1–2" (2.5–5 cm) long; pod is elliptical and erect

Bloom: spring, summer

Cycle/Origin: perennial; native

Habitat: dry to moist acid soils, bogs, low pinewoods, shade

Range: throughout North Carolina, northwestern South Carolina

Notes: Also called Moccasin Flower. Found in large colonies in mountain pinewoods and in bogs near the North Carolina coast. One of the largest orchids in the Carolinas, it produces only one flower (rarely two) per stalk. Flower is usually a deep rosy pink (sometimes white), turning pale pink with age. Small bees enter flower through a slit running the length of the slipper. Once inside, the bee can't back out, so it proceeds toward two escape holes at the top of the slipper, picking up a pollen sac along the way, which is deposited in the next orchid. Please do not attempt to transplant.

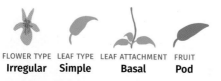

FLOWER TYPE	LEAF TYPE	LEAF ATTACHMENT	FRUIT
Irregular	**Simple**	**Basal**	**Pod**

Pinkladies
Oenothera speciosa

Family: Evening Primrose (Onagraceae)

Height: 8–24" (20–61 cm)

Flower: pink, 2–3" (5–7.5 cm) wide, bowl-shaped, 4 broadly heart-shaped overlapping petals with darker pink veins, shallowly notched on outer edge; yellow center ringed with white; solitary flower attaches directly to each upper leaf junction (axis)

Leaf: lance-shaped or oval, 1–3" (2.5–7.5 cm) long, smooth margin, shallowly toothed or deeply cleft pointed lobes; multiple stems

Fruit: slim green pod, turning brown, ½–1" (1–2.5 cm) long, club-shaped, 4-sided, lengthwise grooves

Bloom: summer

Cycle/Origin: perennial; non-native

Habitat: dry soils, disturbed sites, lawns, fallow fields, sun

Range: throughout the Carolinas, except in the western mountainous counties

Notes: Also called Showy Evening Primrose, for the delicate-looking, shell-pink flowers. Despite its fragile appearance, the plant is fairly heat and drought tolerant. Although in the Evening Primrose family, the flowers are open only in daylight and are pollinated by day-flying insects. Originating in Mexico and the Southwest, this pretty bloom is widely cultivated and has naturalized over much of the southern U.S. Spreads by creeping roots. Can be invasive, overtaking gardens.

FLOWER TYPE	LEAF TYPE	LEAF TYPE	LEAF ATTACHMENT	FRUIT
Regular	**Simple**	**Simple Lobed**	**Alternate**	**Pod**

Henbit Deadnettle
Lamium amplexicaule

Family: Mint (Lamiaceae)

Height: 6–16" (15–40 cm)

Flower: round cluster, 2–3" (5–7.5 cm) wide, of 4–5 pink-to-purple flowers; each flower, 1" (2.5 cm) long, made up of 1 dark pink, hairy, protruding upper lobe and 2 light pink lower lobes with dark rose spots

Leaf: rounded or fan-shaped, lobed, 1" (2.5 cm) wide, 5 lobes, bluntly toothed, green with purple edges, upper surface very wrinkled; upper leaves stalkless, attaching just below flowers; lower leaves stalked; square hollow green stem with purplish base

Bloom: spring, summer

Cycle/Origin: annual, biennial; non-native

Habitat: dry soils, old fields, disturbed sites, parks, sun

Range: throughout

Notes: Like other members of the Mint family, the flower of Henbit Deadnettle looks somewhat like a tiny orchid. Unlike other mints, its leaves and stems do not have the characteristic minty fragrance when crushed. Introduced from Europe and the Mediterranean to the southern states for erosion control, this short plant has become an invasive weed throughout the United States. It can grow plantlets from pieces of the stem, thus when it is tilled under with the soil, it often forms large populations that cover entire fields with a colorful pink carpet of flowers.

CLUSTER TYPE
Round

FLOWER TYPE
Irregular

LEAF TYPE
Simple Lobed

LEAF ATTACHMENT
Opposite

fruit

Clasping Milkweed
Asclepias amplexicaulis

Family: Milkweed (Asclepiadaceae)

Height: 8–36" (20–91 cm)

Flower: loose round or cylindrical cluster, 2–5½" (5–14 cm) wide, of 18–60 pink flowers; each flower, ½" (1 cm) wide, crown of 5 scoop-shaped petals ("hoods") and 5 inward-curving pointed petals ("horns"), 5 downward-pointing lobes; single cluster per plant

Leaf: broadly oval, 3–6" (7.5–15 cm) long, dark green, blunt ends, deeply wavy margin

Fruit: okra-shaped curved green seedpod, turning reddish green, 4–5" (10–13 cm) long, splits along 1 side to release many flattened seeds; each seed attached to white hair-like fuzz that becomes airborne

Bloom: summer

Cycle/Origin: perennial; native

Habitat: dry sandy soils, old fields, open woods, roadsides

Range: throughout

Notes: Erect unopened seedpods at the top of the stem resemble slightly curved, reddish candles on a candelabrum. American Indians used the hair-like fuzz from ripe pods as diaper padding. Also known as Bluntleaf Milkweed, this plant can be differentiated from other milkweed species by its very wavy leaves that clasp the stalk. The single reddish green stem is unbranched, hollow and exudes a milky sap when cut.

CLUSTER TYPE	FLOWER TYPE	LEAF TYPE	LEAF ATTACHMENT	LEAF ATTACHMENT	FRUIT
Round	**Irregular**	**Simple**	**Opposite**	**Clasping**	**Pod**

Obedient Plant
Physostegia virginiana

Family: Mint (Lamiaceae)

Height: 1–5' (30–152 cm)

Flower: dense spike cluster, 2–6" (5–15 cm) long, of pink, lavender or white flowers; each flower, ½–1" (1–2.5 cm) long, made up of wrinkled petals fused to form tube with 2 flaring lips; 3-lobed lower lip has purple spots; throat opening almost rectangular; cone-shaped green calyx with crown-like top

Leaf: slim, lance-shaped, 1–7" (2.5–18 cm) long, pointed tip, sharply toothed edges, oppositely attached, stalkless; smooth 4-angled hollow stem

Bloom: summer, fall

Cycle/Origin: perennial; native

Habitat: moist to wet soils, disturbed sites, stream banks, bogs, seepages, meadows, along railroads, sun

Range: throughout

Notes: "Obedient" is for the flowers, which remain in whatever position they are placed. The spike blooms from the bottom up, with new flowers continuing to open even after it is cut. Native to states north of the Carolinas, this commonly cultivated flower is quite aggressive and has naturalized throughout the southeastern United States. Often planted in butterfly gardens and a favorite of hummingbirds. It is easily grown in moist, well-drained soil in full sun. Numerous commercial cultivars are available for landscape use.

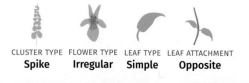

CLUSTER TYPE	FLOWER TYPE	LEAF TYPE	LEAF ATTACHMENT
Spike	**Irregular**	**Simple**	**Opposite**

Mountain Laurel

Kalmia latifolia

Family: Heath (Ericaceae)

Height: 3–15' (.9–4.6 m); shrub

Flower: round cluster, 3–5" (7.5–13 cm) wide, of star-shaped pink (fading to white) flowers; each flower, ¾–1" (2–2.5 cm) wide, 5 pointed petals fused together to form a cup, very long flower parts protrude from center; cluster grows near the top of a woody stalk

Leaf: elliptical, 2–5" (5–13 cm) long and ¾–1½" (2–4 cm) wide, leathery, glossy dark green, pointed tip, margin rolling under, hairless; 2-edged reddish stem; evergreen leaves often clustered at top of stem

Bloom: spring, summer

Cycle/Origin: perennial; native

Habitat: rocky or sandy acid soils, bluffs, bogs, along streams

Range: throughout South Carolina, western two-thirds of North Carolina

Notes: A woody shrub, commonly forming dense thickets on hillsides and in the mountains. The shade produced by these thickets provides protection to several rare plants of the Appalachians. The flowers, twigs and hairless leaves are poisonous—even honey made from the nectar may be toxic. Flower parts are fused until visiting bees bump against them, triggering an explosive release of the mature pollen. Genus name *Kalmia* honors Swedish botanist Peter Kalm. Makes a great landscape planting or specimen, especially for borders. More than 80 cultivated varieties, which have a range of flower colors.

CLUSTER TYPE	FLOWER TYPE	LEAF TYPE	LEAF ATTACHMENT
Round	**Regular**	**Simple**	**Alternate**

Heartwing Sorrel

Rumex hastatulus

Family: Buckwheat (Polygonaceae)

Height: 12–36" (30–91 cm)

Flower: spike cluster, 4–12" (10–30 cm) long, of multiple erect branches of numerous, densely packed, tiny flowers; flowers are green, turning pink, then red

Leaf: many basal, arrowhead-shaped, 3–7" (7.5–18 cm) long, deeply divided into 3 lobes, middle lobe much longer than the others; fewer stem leaves

Fruit: heart-shaped green pod, ⅛" (.3 cm) wide, rimmed with pink or red

Bloom: spring

Cycle/Origin: perennial; native

Habitat: moist to dry sandy soils, disturbed sites, sun

Range: throughout South Carolina, eastern half of North Carolina

Notes: Also called Wild Dock, this plant has a sour taste and is poisonous when consumed in large amounts. More than a dozen plants in this genus in the Carolinas, some native and some introduced. *Hastulus* is Latin and means "spear-shaped," referring to the shape of the leaves. "Heartwing" refers to the seeds, which are two heart-shaped structures set back-to-back and bent at right angles to each other. Abandoned pastures near the coast often look pinkish orange and purple in early spring with a mixture of blooming Heartwing Sorrel and Texas Toadflax (pg. 179) or Canada Toadflax (pg. 137).

CLUSTER TYPE	FLOWER TYPE	LEAF TYPE	LEAF ATTACHMENT	LEAF ATTACHMENT	FRUIT
Spike	**Regular**	**Simple Lobed**	**Alternate**	**Basal**	**Pod**

Tuberous Grasspink

Calopogon tuberosus

Family: Orchid (Orchidaceae)

Height: 12–24" (30–61 cm)

Flower: spike cluster, 4–16" (10–40 cm) long, of 3–15 pink-to-magenta flowers; each flower, 1½" (4 cm) wide, of 3 pointed elliptical sepals and 3 petals (1 is a modified lip that has white-, yellow- and magenta-tipped hairs); dark-tipped center column of flower parts protrudes and curves inward

Leaf: narrow, grass-like, 4–20" (10–50 cm) long; usually 1 blade (sometimes 2) per plant

Fruit: elliptical green pod, turning brown, 1" (2.5 cm) long, contains thousands of microscopic seeds that can be seen collectively as a mass

Bloom: spring, summer

Cycle/Origin: perennial; native

Habitat: acid bogs, pond edges, roadsides, meadows, woods

Range: throughout

Notes: Of the five orchid species in the *Calopogon* genus in the Southeast, this is the tallest and has the largest flower. The hairy lip resembles stamens with pollen, fooling bumblebees. The bee lands, setting off a chain reaction—the lip bends from the bee's weight and the bee tumbles against the column, breaking off an anther cap below which the real pollen is hidden. Unwittingly, the bee gets pollen on its back, carrying it away to pollinate another flower.

CLUSTER TYPE	FLOWER TYPE	LEAF TYPE	LEAF ATTACHMENT	LEAF ATTACHMENT	FRUIT
Spike	**Irregular**	**Simple**	**Basal**	**Clasping**	**Pod**

Great Laurel
Rhododendron maximum

Family: Heath (Ericaceae)

Height: 6–32' (1.8–9.8 m); shrub

Flower: dense round cluster, 5–8" (13–20 cm) wide, of 15–30 pale (sometimes dark) pink-to-white flowers; each cup-shaped flower, 1½" (4 cm) wide, 5 blunt- or round-tipped overlapping petals fused at lower ends into very short tube; uppermost petal densely spotted inside with yellowish green or orange

Leaf: oblong to oval, 4–8" (10–20 cm) long, leathery, evergreen, dark green and smooth above, paler with rust-colored hairs below, sharply pointed tip, tapering to wedge at base, stout woody stem

Fruit: elliptical reddish brown capsule, ¾" (2 cm) long, splits along 5 lines to release seeds

Bloom: spring, summer

Cycle/Origin: perennial; native

Habitat: acid soils, woods, bogs, swamps, moist hills, shade

Range: western third of North Carolina, a few western mountainous counties of South Carolina

Notes: The tallest of the rhododendrons in both states, this multi-branched large shrub or small tree provides shelter for many unique plants found in the moist hilly woods in the Appalachians. Most common in the mountains, often growing in dense colonies. All of the plant parts (even honey made from the nectar) are poisonous.

CLUSTER TYPE	FLOWER TYPE	LEAF TYPE	LEAF ATTACHMENT	FRUIT
Round	**Regular**	**Simple**	**Alternate**	**Pod**

Rosepink

Sabatia angularis

Family: Gentian (Gentianaceae)

Height: 8–36" (20–91 cm)

Flower: very loose flat cluster, 5–10" (13–25 cm) wide, of pink (rarely white) flowers; each flower, 1–1½" (2.5–4 cm) wide, of 5 petals spaced around a star-shaped green-and-yellow (sometimes edged with red) center; each flower on tall flower stalk

Leaf: lance-shaped or oval, 1–2" (2.5–5 cm) long, broadest at base; each pair of leaves rotated at right angles to next pair; square, multi-branched, sharply angled stem with slight wings on the angles

Bloom: summer, fall

Cycle/Origin: annual; native

Habitat: upland woods, meadows, stream banks, roadsides, abandoned fields, freshwater or brackish marshes

Range: throughout

Notes: Rosepink tolerates growing in a variety of habitats and is underused as a cultivated garden plant. Its pleasantly fragrant bloom makes a good cut flower—however, please don't pick it from the wild. Also called Bitterbloom, the entire plant was once used in a tonic to treat intestinal worms and fever. One of several other pink-flowered gentians in the Carolinas. The biennial Narrowleaf Rose Gentian (*S. brachiata*) (not shown) is the most similar to Rose Gentian, but it has a round stem rising from a rosette of basal leaves and is found in only the eastern half of the Carolinas.

CLUSTER TYPE	FLOWER TYPE	LEAF TYPE	LEAF ATTACHMENT	LEAF ATTACHMENT	LEAF ATTACHMENT
Flat	**Regular**	**Simple**	**Opposite**	**Perfoliate**	**Clasping**

Sweetscented Joe-pye Weed
Eutrochium purpureum

Family: Aster (Asteraceae)

Height: 2–7' (.6–2.1 m)

Flower: round cluster, 5–10" (13–25 cm) wide, made up of hundreds of dull purplish pink flower heads; each tiny composite flower, ¼" (.6 cm) wide, composed of all disk flowers (no ray flowers)

Leaf: lance-shaped, 3–9" (7.5–23 cm) long, coarse-toothed margin; whorl of 3–5 leaves; leaves smell of vanilla when crushed; green stem (often purplish at leaf attachment) with small white hairs

Bloom: summer, fall

Cycle/Origin: perennial; native

Habitat: dry to wet rich soils, thickets, open woods, sun

Range: throughout

Notes: A tall and robust plant that likes dry soil in thickets and open coniferous and deciduous woods in the uplands. Rare near the coast, it is one of several similar species of joe-pye in the Carolinas. Often confused with Spotted Joe-pye Weed (*Eutrochium maculatum*) (not shown), which has flat clusters and spots on its hairy stems. Look for the green stems with purple at the nodes to distinguish Sweetscented Joe-pye Weed from Trumpetweed (pg. 135), which has hollow stems that are purple or purplish green all over. Named for Joe Pye, an American Indian medicine man. The flowers are a magnet for butterflies. A wonderful perennial available for purchase at many garden centers.

CLUSTER TYPE
Round

FLOWER TYPE
Composite

LEAF TYPE
Simple

LEAF ATTACHMENT
Whorl

Eustis Lake Beardtongue

Penstemon australis

Family: Snapdragon (Scrophulariaceae)

Height: 8–24" (20–61 cm)

Flower: loose spike cluster, 6–7" (15–18 cm) long, of pink flowers; each flower, 1" (2.5 cm) long, of 2-lobed pink upper and 3-lobed white lower petals (lips); dark rose streaks inside; 5 flower parts (1 has brushy yellow tip or "beard"); flower and flower stalk have tiny translucent hairs

Leaf: basal, pointed oval, 2–5" (5–13 cm) long, red veins, on a stalk; stem leaf, arrowhead-shaped; irregular teeth; reddish green, turning burgundy; leaves and sticky purplish red stem covered with tiny hairs

Bloom: summer

Cycle/Origin: perennial; native

Habitat: old pastures, roadsides, burned areas, pinelands

Range: throughout South Carolina, eastern half of North Carolina

Notes: "Beardtongue" is for the hairy sterile fifth flower part (stamen) that projects farther beyond the lower lip of the flower than do the other stamens. This "beard" attracts bumblebees seeking pollen, and in turn, the bees inadvertently pollinate the flower. Hummingbirds and butterflies visit this flower for its nectar, so this is a good plant for wildlife gardens. Other beard-tongues in the genus *Penstemon* in the Carolinas are not as hairy as this species.

CLUSTER TYPE
Spike

FLOWER TYPE
Irregular

LEAF TYPE
Simple

LEAF ATTACHMENT
Opposite

LEAF ATTACHMENT
Basal

LEAF ATTACHMENT
Clasping

Pink Azalea

Rhododendron periclymenoides

Family: Heath (Ericaceae)

Height: 3–6' (.9–1.8 m); shrub

Flower: dense round cluster, 7–8" (18–20 cm) wide, of 7–14 translucent pale pink-to-white (can be variable) flowers; each flower, 1½–2" (4–5 cm) wide, 5 slightly downward-curving, long wavy petals fused into short hairy tube; very long flower parts (stamens)

Leaf: narrow, oblong, 2–4" (5–10 cm) long, small hairs on margin; multi-branched stems; deciduous

Fruit: dark reddish violet capsule, ½–¾" (1–2 cm) long, hairy, contains many pale reddish orange seeds

Bloom: spring, summer

Cycle/Origin: perennial; native

Habitat: open oak-hickory or beech woods, stream banks

Range: throughout the Carolinas, except along the South Carolina coast

Notes: From above, cluster looks like a wagon wheel with long red tufts protruding from the outer rim. The most common rhododendron in South Carolina except along the coast, where Swamp Azalea (pg. 269) is more common. Can be confused with Mountain Azalea *(R. canescens)* (not shown), found in southern South Carolina, but the flower tube of Mountain Azalea is sticky. Flowers in spring before its leaves have emerged or are fully formed. Slightly fragrant blooms attract hummingbirds and insects. Also called Pinxterflower.

CLUSTER TYPE	FLOWER TYPE	LEAF TYPE	LEAF ATTACHMENT	FRUIT
Round	**Regular**	**Simple**	**Alternate**	**Pod**

Trumpetweed

Eutrochium fistulosum

Family: Aster (Asteraceae)

Height: 2–7' (.6–2.1 m)

Flower: large oval or domed round cluster, 12" (30 cm) long and 8" (20 cm) wide, of hundreds of deep pink flower heads; each flower head made up of disk flowers (no ray flowers) with a reddish pink base; 4–7 flower heads per stalk; multi-branched red flower stalks

Leaf: elliptical, 3–10" (7.5–25 cm) long, blunt-toothed margin, rough; whorls of 4–7 leaves around hollow purple or purplish green stem

Bloom: summer, fall

Cycle/Origin: perennial; native

Habitat: wet meadows, moist woods, bogs, marshes, sun

Range: western two-thirds of the Carolinas

Notes: Trumpetweed is a wetland plant that can grow as tall as 10 feet (3 m). This vanilla-scented wildflower is also known as Hollow Joe-pye Weed for its unique hollow stem, unlike the solid stems of the many species of joe-pye weed in the Carolinas. Related to Sweetscented Joe-pye Weed (pg. 129), which has green stems and round flower clusters that are dull purplish pink. The dried brown seed heads remain on the stems, looking dramatic well into fall. The impressive flower clusters are a magnet for butterflies and other pollinators.

CLUSTER TYPE **Round**   FLOWER TYPE **Composite**   LEAF TYPE **Simple**   LEAF ATTACHMENT **Whorl**

Canada Toadflax
Nuttallanthus canadensis

Family: Snapdragon (Scrophulariaceae)

Height: 8–18" (20–45 cm)

Flower: purple to blue, ¼–½" (.6–1 cm) long, made of petals forming 2 lips; 2-lobed, erect upper lip; 3-lobed larger lower lip with raised white throat; curved or straight spur; flowers grouped at top of stem; only a few flowers bloom at a time

Leaf: mostly stem leaves alternately attached along lower half of stem; very thin, basal, ⅔–1½" (1.6–4 cm) long, pointed tip, attached in a rosette at base

Bloom: early spring, summer

Cycle/Origin: annual, biennial; native

Habitat: dry shallow rocky or sandy soils, disturbed sites, roadsides, old fields, sun

Range: throughout the Carolinas, except in the western mountainous counties of North Carolina

Notes: Canada Toadflax has a smaller flower and shorter nectar spur than the similar Texas Toadflax (pg. 179). The foliage is food for Common Buckeye butterfly caterpillars. Pollinated mostly by bumblebees, although butterflies do visit the flowers for the nectar. An important nectar source for honeybees, because the flowers bloom early in spring and in large masses. Only a few flowers on each plant bloom at one time. Plants produce copious amounts of seed and are aggressive colonizers of disturbed sites.

FLOWER TYPE	LEAF TYPE	LEAF ATTACHMENT	LEAF ATTACHMENT
Irregular	**Simple**	**Alternate**	**Basal**

Clasping Venus' Looking-glass
Triodanis perfoliata

Family: Bellflower (Campanulaceae)

Height: 6–36" (15–91 cm)

Flower: bluish purple to lavender (can be bright blue), ⅓–⅝" (.8–1.5 cm) wide, star-shaped, made up of 5 oblong pointed petals (sometimes streaked with white) around a paler center

Leaf: heart-shaped, ¼–1" (.6–2.5 cm) long, rounded tip, blunt-toothed margin; upper leaves much smaller than lower; densely leafy, 5-angled, deeply grooved stem with white hairs

Bloom: spring, summer

Cycle/Origin: annual; native

Habitat: dry sandy soils, disturbed areas, gardens, woods

Range: throughout

Notes: Also called Roundleaf Triodanis or Clasping Bellflower, with both names referring to the rounded leaves that clasp the stem. Although in the Bellflower family, the petals are horizontal or slightly erect, not fused together into a bell shape and hanging downward, as is typical of those in the family. Like others in the Triodanis genus, the upper flowers open for pollination, while the lower flowers stay closed and are self-pollinating. Attracts small butterflies, bees and flies. A similar wildflower, the American Bellflower (*Campanulastrum americanum*) (not shown), occurs in western North Carolina and has larger flowers than those of this plant.

FLOWER TYPE
Regular

LEAF TYPE
Simple

LEAF ATTACHMENT
Alternate

LEAF ATTACHMENT
Clasping

Rice Button Aster
Symphyotrichum dumosum

Family: Aster (Asteraceae)

Height: 12–36" (30–91 cm)

Flower: lavender-to-pale blue-to-white flower head, ½–¾" (1–2 cm) wide, made up of 13–30 petals (ray flowers) around an orangish yellow center (disk flowers); center turns reddish brown when pollinated; flower heads grow on long thin arching flower stalks with bract-like leaves

Leaf: lance-shaped, 1–4½" (2.5–11 cm) long, rough to the touch above, stalkless; hairy upper stem

Bloom: summer, fall

Cycle/Origin: perennial; native

Habitat: disturbed sites, old fields, gravel banks, sun

Range: throughout

Notes: The many branching flower stalks with bract-like leaves appear feather-like or asparagus fern-like, thus it is also called Bushy Aster. Hairy White Oldfield Aster (pg. 227) is similar to Rice Button Aster, but its flowers are usually white, and it is not nearly as bushy. The blooms of both of these species attract butterflies. Widely cultivated, Rice Button Aster makes a great addition to fall bouquets of cut flowers. Serves as a larval host plant for the Pearl Crescent butterfly.

FLOWER TYPE **Composite**   LEAF TYPE **Simple**   LEAF ATTACHMENT **Alternate**

Field Pansy
Viola bicolor

Family: Violet (Violaceae)

Height: 2–16" (5–40 cm)

Flower: variable in color (can be purple, blue, pink, cream or white), ½–¾" (1–2 cm) wide, with a yellow-and-white throat; 5 unequal-sized petals; lower 3 petals streaked with purple; single flowers on flower stalks

Leaf: basal, round or oval, ½" (1 cm) wide, edges shallowly notched, stalked; larger spoon-shaped stem leaf; large, deeply lobed, leaf-like stipules ring stem at each leaf axis; multi-branched stem

Bloom: spring, summer

Cycle/Origin: annual; native

Habitat: dry to moist sandy soils, pastures, lawns, along railroads, fencerows, disturbed sites, woods, sun

Range: throughout

Notes: Also known as Johnny-jump-up for its rapid growth and sudden appearance in the spring. This wildflower reproduces mainly by seed and can be found in large colonies, especially along roads. It is one of more than 20 species of violet in the Carolinas, and hybrids are common, making identification difficult. More heat resistant than the common garden pansy, Field Pansy is readily available at garden centers. Plants in the Violet family are host plants for fritillary butterfly caterpillars. This species is quite aggressive and can quickly invade garden spaces.

FLOWER TYPE
Irregular

LEAF TYPE
Simple

LEAF ATTACHMENT
Alternate

LEAF ATTACHMENT
Basal

Curtiss' Milkwort

Polygala curtissii

Family: Milkwort (Polygalaceae)

Height: 4–16" (10–40 cm)

Flower: cylindrical spike cluster, ½–1" (1–2.5 cm) long, of lavender-to-pink flowers; each flower, ¼" (.6 cm) long, 3 fused lavender or white petals tipped with yellow, 5 purple-rose or bright pink sepals (2 form spreading "wings"); top of cluster blunt or pointed due to unopened yellow buds; spiny bracts stay on stalk after flowers finish blooming

Leaf: very narrow and oblong, ½–1" (1–2.5 cm) long, smooth margin, pointed tip; leaves alternately attached to branching stem

Bloom: summer, fall

Cycle/Origin: annual; native

Habitat: dry to moist sandy soils, abandoned pastures, thickets, clearings, disturbed sites, woodland edges, sun

Range: western two-thirds of the Carolinas

Notes: Also known as Appalachian Milkwort. This species most closely resembles two uncommon relatives in the Carolinas, Purple Milkwort *(P. sanguinea)* and Drumheads *(P. cruciata)* (neither shown), which have much more tightly packed flower clusters and lack yellow on the open flowers. Genus name *Polygala* is Greek and means "much milk," referring to the belief that these plants increased the amount of milk produced by cows and nursing human mothers.

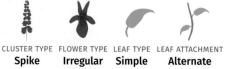

CLUSTER TYPE **Spike** FLOWER TYPE **Irregular** LEAF TYPE **Simple** LEAF ATTACHMENT **Alternate**

Three-lobe Violet

Viola palmata

Family: Violet (Violaceae)

Height: 4–6" (10–15 cm)

Flower: variable in color (can be deep violet, purple, blue, white or white streaked with purple), 1" (2.5 cm) wide, with a bearded white throat; made up of 5 unequal-sized petals; nodding flower on its own hairy reddish flower stalk

Leaf: basal, lobed, 2½" (6 cm) long, deeply divided into 3–11 toothed lobes, dark green above, light green and hairy along veins below, on long stalk

Bloom: spring

Cycle/Origin: perennial; native

Habitat: dry upland woods, rocky bluffs, meadows

Range: throughout

Notes: The many different shapes of the leaves and the wide range of flower colors make this one of the most variable of the violets. Now thought to be a hybrid between any two of four violet species, which may account for some of its lack of consistency in appearance. Species name *palmata* refers to some of the lobed leaves resembling the fingers and palm of the human hand. However, the first leaves to emerge are often heart-shaped or oval and only slightly toothed or have smooth edges. The similar Bird's Foot Violet (pg. 33) has even more deeply cleft leaves than those of Three-lobe Violet.

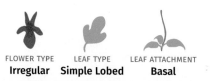

FLOWER TYPE
Irregular

LEAF TYPE
Simple Lobed

LEAF ATTACHMENT
Basal

Sharpwing Monkeyflower
Mimulus alatus

Family: Snapdragon (Scrophulariaceae)

Height: 2–4' (61–122 cm)

Flower: lavender, 1" (2.5 cm) long, 2 petals (lips); hairy, 2-lobed, erect upper lip folding backward; lower lip of 3 unequal-sized, rounded, broad horizontal lobes; yellow beard on lower middle lobe; whitish throat

Leaf: broad and lance-shaped, 2–5" (5–13 cm) long, pointed tip, blunt- to coarse-toothed margin; lower leaves on stalks, upper leaves almost stalkless; each opposite pair at right angles to previous pair

Fruit: cylindrical brown pod, ½" (1 cm) long, smooth

Bloom: summer

Cycle/Origin: perennial; native

Habitat: marshes, woods, ditches, bottomlands, seepages

Range: southeastern half of South Carolina, eastern two-thirds of North Carolina

Notes: Named for the face of the flower, which some think resembles that of a grinning monkey. The lower petals form a landing platform for bumblebees and other insect pollinators, with the yellow beard guiding them into the flower. Regularly cross-pollinates with Allegheny Monkeyflower (*M. ringens*) (not shown), producing hybrids. Look for the leafstalks on the lower leaves to differentiate it from Allegheny Monkeyflower, which has stalkless leaves. Rarely, a white-flowering Sharpwing Monkeyflower is ever found.

FLOWER TYPE **Irregular** LEAF TYPE **Simple** LEAF ATTACHMENT **Opposite** FRUIT **Pod**

Purple False Foxglove
Agalinis purpurea

Family: Snapdragon (Scrophulariaceae)

Height: 12–36" (30–91 cm)

Flower: purple to pink, 1" (2.5 cm) long, trumpet-shaped, made of 5 lobed petals fused halfway along their length to form tube, flaring widely at mouth; 2 yellowish streaks and pink or purple spots inside the whitish throat; 6–14 flowers grouped on stalk

Leaf: narrowly lance-shaped, 1–3" (2.5–7.5 cm) long, dark green, smooth, short stalk; square stems and leaves often purple tinted; leaves often missing or smaller toward top of branching or single stem

Fruit: round green pod, turning brown, ¼" (.6 cm) wide

Bloom: summer, fall

Cycle/Origin: annual; native

Habitat: moist sandy soils, disturbed areas, roadsides, pond banks, fields, moist woods, sun

Range: throughout

Notes: One of only 14 species of purple false foxglove in the Carolinas, this plant is difficult to distinguish from the other false foxgloves with purple flowers. It derives some of its nutrients from other plants (hemiparasitic), inserting its roots into those of native grasses, Loblolly Pines or sycamore or sweetgum trees. Caterpillars of the pretty Common Buckeye butterfly eat the foliage, making the plant an attractive choice for wildlife landscapes.

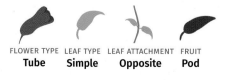

FLOWER TYPE	LEAF TYPE	LEAF ATTACHMENT	FRUIT
Tube	**Simple**	**Opposite**	**Pod**

Spotted Geranium

Geranium maculatum

Family: Geranium (Geraniaceae)

Height: 12–24" (30–61 cm)

Flower: lavender or pink, 1–2" (2.5–5 cm) wide, made up of 5 heavily veined, rounded petals, groups of 2–10 flowers top the stem

Leaf: basal, lobed, 4–5" (10–13 cm) long, divided into 5–7 elongated lobes, deeply veined, coarse-toothed margin, on long stalk; only 2–3 stem leaves (sparsely covered with white hairs) per plant

Fruit: elongated beak-like green capsule, turning dark reddish brown, 1–1½" (2.5–4 cm) long, splitting lengthwise to release many seeds

Bloom: spring, summer

Cycle/Origin: perennial; native

Habitat: moist rocky rich soils, open deciduous woods, meadows, shade

Range: western two-thirds of the Carolinas

Notes: A common spring-blooming perennial of shady deciduous woodlands, Spotted Geranium is rare near the coast. Its delicate lavender or pink flowers rise above its many-lobed leaves. The seed capsule opens to release seeds by splitting into five long, curled, banana-like "peels." Genus name *Geranium* comes from the Greek *geranos* for "crane," because the seed capsule's long narrow shape is like that of the bill of a crane. Also called Carolina Crane's Bill.

FLOWER TYPE	LEAF TYPE	LEAF ATTACHMENT	LEAF ATTACHMENT	FRUIT
Regular	**Simple Lobed**	**Opposite**	**Basal**	**Pod**

Carolina Wild Petunia

Ruellia caroliniensis

Family: Acanthus (Acanthaceae)

Height: 12–36" (30–91 cm)

Flower: lavender to purple, 1–2" (2.5–5 cm) long, trumpet-shaped, 5 fused petals forming a long tube and then spreading widely at mouth into rounded lobes; hairy sepals (calyx); 1 to several erect flowers grow at leaf attachments; often occur in pairs

Leaf: oval, 1½–5" (4–13 cm) long, oppositely attached to hairy stem

Fruit: oval green capsule, turning red, ½" (1 cm) long, smooth

Bloom: summer, fall

Cycle/Origin: perennial; native

Habitat: dry to moist sandy soils, old fields, disturbed areas, woods, thickets, sun

Range: throughout

Notes: Named for the Carolinas, where it is common, but this pretty wildflower is also found in many other states. Although "Petunia" is the latter part of the common name, it is a member of the Acanthus family and is not actually a petunia, which belongs to the Nightshade family. Also called Hairy Ruellia for the hairs on the stems. Often found blooming in areas where there has been a recent fire. Hummingbirds are attracted to the nectar of the showy flowers. Occasionally considered a lawn and yard weed.

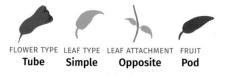

FLOWER TYPE	LEAF TYPE	LEAF ATTACHMENT	FRUIT
Tube	**Simple**	**Opposite**	**Pod**

Southern Swamp Aster

Eurybia paludosa

Family: Aster (Asteraceae)

Height: 8–36" (20–91 cm)

Flower: deep lavender-to-pale purple flower head, 1–2" (2.5–5 cm) wide, of 15–35 narrow petals (ray flowers) around 25–30 tubular yellow disk flowers; 4-10 flowers at each leaf axis, 1 above the other on stalk

Leaf: basal, narrow and grass-like, 2–8" (5–20 cm) long, smooth margin, stalked; stem leaf, on shorter stalk or stalkless, widely spaced along orangish stem

Bloom: summer, fall

Cycle/Origin: perennial; native

Habitat: open low pinewoods, edges of swamps and springs

Range: eastern half of the Carolinas

Notes: As its name implies, Southern Swamp Aster is a wetland-loving species that usually grows in moist to wet soils and flowers from late summer through fall. Native to and found only in the Atlantic coastal area, it sometimes grows in drier sandy hills of the coastal plain. This tall slender plant has narrow grass-like leaves concentrated at the base. There are relatively few leaves widely spaced along the stem.

FLOWER TYPE **Composite**   LEAF TYPE **Simple**   LEAF ATTACHMENT **Alternate**   LEAF ATTACHMENT **Basal**   LEAF ATTACHMENT **Clasping**

Wild Bergamot
Monarda fistulosa

Family: Mint (Lamiaceae)

Height: 2–4' (61–122 cm)

Flower: round cluster, 1–2" (2.5–5 cm) wide, of many pale lavender flowers; each flower, 1" (2.5 cm) long, 2 petals (lips), upper lip tipped with tuft of hairs; clusters top the stems and branches

Leaf: lance-shaped, 1–3" (2.5–7.5 cm) long, tapering to pointed tip, coarse-toothed margin, short leafstalk; oppositely attached to square red stem

Bloom: summer, fall

Cycle/Origin: perennial; native

Habitat: dry to moist soils, old fields, moist wooded slopes, forest edges, roadsides, sun

Range: western and central North Carolina, western and central South Carolina

Notes: Also called Horsemint or Bee Balm, this is a tall plant of dry woods, forest margins, open areas and roadsides. Look for its square stems and oppositely attached leaves to help identify. Emits a strong scent when any part of the plant is rubbed or crushed. The fragrance of the flower heads attracts many insects, including bees, butterflies and beetles. "Bergamot" refers to a small citrus tree that produces a scent similar to that of this plant. Once used in folk medicine to make a mint tea to treat many respiratory and digestive ailments. Its oil is an essential flavoring in Earl Grey tea.

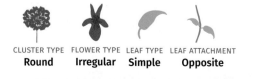

CLUSTER TYPE
Round

FLOWER TYPE
Irregular

LEAF TYPE
Simple

LEAF ATTACHMENT
Opposite

American Hog-peanut

Amphicarpaea bracteata

Family: Pea or Bean (Fabaceae)

Height: 1–5' (30–152 cm); vine

Flower: drooping loose round cluster, 1–2" (2.5–5 cm) wide, of 2 to many lavender-to-white (or cream) flowers; each tubular flower, ⅝" (1.5 cm) long

Leaf: compound, 6" (15 cm) long, of 3 diamond-shaped to oval leaflets; each leaflet, 1–4" (2.5–10 cm) long, rounded base, on long stalk; hairy twining stem

Fruit: produces 2 types: pea-pod-shaped green capsule, turning brown, ⅝–1½" (1.5–4 cm) long, hairy along seams, pointed base and tip, contains 3–4 seeds; juicy closed fruit (the hog-peanut), contains 1 seed

Bloom: summer, fall

Cycle/Origin: annual, perennial; native

Habitat: woods, ravines, slopes, roadsides, sun to shade

Range: throughout

Notes: Upper flowers open and are pollinated by insects, while lower flowers are on creeping or underground vines, never open and self-pollinate. Both types produce seeds, but the lower flowers each produce a one-seeded juicy closed fruit called a hog-peanut. American Indians prized the fruit and root as food, but avoided eating seeds of the upper flowers. Currently cultivated to fix nitrogen into the soil, thus improving soil fertility. Golden-banded Skipper and Southern Cloudywing butterfly caterpillars eat the foliage.

CLUSTER TYPE
Round

FLOWER TYPE
Tube

LEAF TYPE
Compound

LEAF ATTACHMENT
Alternate

FRUIT
Pod

Alfalfa

Medicago sativa

Family: Pea or Bean (Fabaceae)

Height: 12–36" (30–91 cm)

Flower: tight spike cluster, 1–2" (2.5–5 cm) long, of deep purple-to-dark blue (can range to light blue) flowers; each flower, ¼–⅓" (.6–.8 cm) long, has 1 large upper petal and 3 smaller lower petals

Leaf: 3-parted and clover-like, 1–2" (2.5–5 cm) long

Fruit: downy green seedpod twists into coils, turning nearly black with age

Bloom: spring, summer, fall

Cycle/Origin: perennial; non-native

Habitat: dry soils, fields, along roads, sun

Range: throughout

Notes: This deep-rooted perennial is usually found along roads or fields where it has escaped cultivation. Alfalfa is often planted by farmers as a food crop for farm animals and to improve soil fertility by fixing nitrogen from air into the soil through its roots. A winter-hardy variety of alfalfa developed in the late 1800s was partially responsible for the establishment of the dairy industry in the upper Midwest in the early 1900s. The thin stems often cause the plant to fall over under its own weight when mature, leaving it prostrate. Alfalfa is a prime larval host for the Orange Sulphur and Clouded Sulphur butterflies. Countless individuals hovering above a field of blooming alfalfa look like a swarm of dancing orange and yellow flowers.

CLUSTER TYPE	FLOWER TYPE	LEAF TYPE	LEAF ATTACHMENT	FRUIT
Spike	**Irregular**	**Compound**	**Alternate**	**Pod**

Hairy Skullcap

Scutellaria elliptica

Family: Mint (Lamiaceae)

Height: 6–36" (15–91 cm)

Flower: open spike cluster, 1¼–4" (3–10 cm) long, of pale lavender flowers; each flower, ⅝–1" (1.5–2.5 cm) long, of 2 petals (lips); hairy darker upper lip forms a "hood" over lower whitish lip with purple spots or stripes; knobbed calyx behind each flower

Leaf: oval, 1½–2¾" (4–7 cm) long, pointed tip, numerous teeth on edges, flat base, on sticky hairy stalk, oppositely attached to square purplish stem

Bloom: spring, summer

Cycle/Origin: perennial; native

Habitat: dry to moist soils, upland woods, old fields

Range: throughout South Carolina, western two-thirds of North Carolina

Notes: "Hairy" in the common name describes the leafstalks and flowers, while "Skullcap" refers to the knobbed calyx, which resembles a close-fitting brimless cap. This plant lacks the minty scent characteristic of many members of the Mint family. The leaf edges of Hairy Skullcap have numerous teeth, unlike those of the middle and upper leaves of the similar Helmet Flower (pg. 175), which are smooth or have just a few small teeth. The distinctive flowers attract a variety of bees and butterflies, making it a good choice for wildlife gardens.

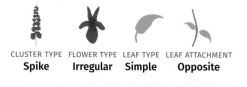

CLUSTER TYPE	FLOWER TYPE	LEAF TYPE	LEAF ATTACHMENT
Spike	**Irregular**	**Simple**	**Opposite**

Spurred Butterfly Pea

Centrosema virginianum

Family: Pea or Bean (Fabaceae)

Height: 2–5' (61–152 cm); vine

Flower: lavender, 1½" (4 cm) wide, made of 5 dissimilarly shaped petals, white streak in center of the 2 broadest joined petals; up to 4 flowers loosely arranged on a short flower stalk attached at each leaf attachment (axis)

Leaf: compound, made up of 3 oval leaflets; each leaflet, 1–3" (2.5–7.5 cm) long, pointed tip; leaf shaped like a turkey's foot; leaves alternately attached to a twining stem

Fruit: long, thin, flat green pod, turning brown, 3–5" (7.5–13 cm) long, stalkless; after releasing seeds, sides of pod tightly curl up and the dry pod remains on vine

Bloom: spring, summer, fall

Cycle/Origin: perennial; native

Habitat: dry sandy soils, open oak-hickory woods or pinewoods, fields, roadsides, coastal dunes, sun

Range: throughout

Notes: This climbing or trailing vine is relatively low growing and often cultivated for its pretty flowers. Like most plants in the Pea or Bean family, Spurred Butterfly Pea has nodules of bacteria on its roots that fix the nitrogen into the soil, thus improving soil fertility for plants. Host for several skipper butterflies.

FLOWER TYPE
Irregular

LEAF TYPE
Compound

LEAF ATTACHMENT
Alternate

FRUIT
Pod

fruit

Purple Passionflower

Passiflora incarnata

Family: Passionflower (Passifloraceae)

Height: 7–26' (2.1–7.9 m); vine

Flower: lavender (can be pink and white), 1½–2½" (4–6 cm) wide, 5 elliptical sepals and 5 similar petals below fringed crown of wavy white or lavender filaments; filaments are around a band of purple or pink that surrounds a green or white center; intricate solitary blooms grow from leaf attachments

Leaf: broad, lobed, 2½–6" (6–15 cm) long, 3 deep lobes, fine-toothed edges; sticky tendril at leaf attachment

Fruit: green pod, turning yellow, 2–3" (5–7.5 cm) long, the shape and size of a chicken's egg, pulpy, fragrant

Bloom: spring, summer

Cycle/Origin: perennial; native

Habitat: disturbed areas, old pastures, deciduous forests, sun

Range: throughout

Notes: This exotic-looking wildflower has many common names, including Maypop, for the popping sounds the pod makes when squashed. American Indians and early settlers ate the fruit or used them in drinks, ate young leaves as greens and used the roots in medicines. The fruit (called passion fruit) are still used in beverages. Planting it in a garden almost guarantees the arrival of the bright orange Gulf Fritillary butterfly, and frequently the Zebra Heliconian, both of which use this plant as a larval host.

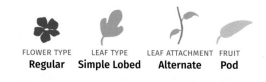

FLOWER TYPE	LEAF TYPE	LEAF ATTACHMENT	FRUIT
Regular	**Simple Lobed**	**Alternate**	**Pod**

Tall Morning Glory

Ipomoea purpurea

Family: Morning Glory (Convolvulaceae)

Height: 12–15' (3.7–4.6 m); vine

Flower: usually deep purple (can be white, pink, blue or variegated), 1½–2½" (4–6 cm) long, with lighter pinkish purple center, trumpet-shaped, the base of trumpet tightly enclosed by very hairy green calyx; 1–5 flowers per flower stalk

Leaf: heart-shaped, 2–5" (5–13 cm) long, on long stalk, alternately attached to a twining red vine that has long white hairs

Fruit: 3-parted spherical greenish pod, turning brown, ½" (1 cm) wide, flattened on each end

Bloom: summer, fall

Cycle/Origin: annual; non-native

Habitat: dry soils, waste sites, roadsides, old fields, gardens, sun to partial shade

Range: throughout

Notes: Introduced from Mexico and Central America to the United States and planted in gardens, this vine has naturalized and spread widely, becoming an invasive weed. Many cultivated varieties with a wide range of flower colors are available for planting and often escape to the wild. All plant parts of Tall Morning Glory are toxic. The seeds contain a hallucinogenic compound and have been used medicinally.

FLOWER TYPE
Tube

LEAF TYPE
Simple

LEAF ATTACHMENT
Alternate

FRUIT
Pod

yellow flower

Horrid Thistle
Cirsium horridulum

Family: Aster (Asteraceae)

Height: 1–5' (30–152 cm)

Flower: pink-purple or white flower (sometimes dull yellow) flower head, 2–3" (5–7.5 cm) wide, disk-shaped, made of thin tubular disk flowers; flower head atop base of very slim, short, erect, extremely spiny bracts; more bracts dangle outward below and circle the base

Leaf: elliptical or lance-shaped, 2–5" (5–13 cm) long, with many lobes, each ending in a spine; basal leaves in a rosette; stem leaves alternately clasping the stem; short thick white-haired stem has few branches

Bloom: summer

Cycle/Origin: biennial; native

Habitat: along ocean shores and salt marshes, disturbed sites

Range: throughout the Carolinas, except in the mountainous western counties

Notes: Horrid Thistle is common in the eastern Carolinas near the coast, while Bull Thistle (pg. 205), which has much slimmer stems, narrower leaves and deep reddish purple flower heads, is more common in the western Carolinas. Butterflies love to drink thistle nectar, and it is timely that thistles bloom just after many butterfly species emerge from their chrysalises. Surprisingly, the miniscule male flower parts (anthers) actually move when touched by an insect, curving toward the intruder and covering it with pollen.

FLOWER TYPE
Composite

LEAF TYPE
Simple Lobed

LEAF ATTACHMENT
Alternate

LEAF ATTACHMENT
Basal

LEAF ATTACHMENT
Clasping

Helmet Flower

Scutellaria integrifolia

Family: Mint (Lamiaceae)

Height: 12–24" (30–61 cm)

Flower: loose spike cluster, 2–8" (5–20 cm) long, of purple-to-pink (can be white) flowers; each tube-shaped flower, ½–1" (1–2.5 cm) long, swollen at midline, fuzzy bulbous upper petal (lip) forms "hood" over broad lower lip with 2 white bands; hairy green sepals (calyx) rimmed with maroon

Leaf: middle and upper, elliptical, 1–2½" (2.5–6 cm) long, edges usually toothless or with small teeth, stalkless; lower, triangular, toothed, stalked; lower leaves drop off early; slightly hairy square stem

Bloom: summer

Cycle/Origin: perennial; native

Habitat: swamps, fields, moist pinewoods, forest seeps

Range: throughout

Notes: Sometimes the flowers never open, self-pollinating and setting seed while closed. The leaves and flowers (when they do open) lack fragrance, unlike most other types of mints. *Scutellaria* is from the Latin word for "dish" or "skullcap" and describes the shape of the maroon-rimmed green calyx, which stays on the plant when it is fruiting. "Helmet" refers to the bulbous upper lip, which has a helmet shape. Differs from all other skullcaps in the Carolinas as the middle and upper leaves have smooth edges or a few small teeth.

CLUSTER TYPE	FLOWER TYPE	LEAF TYPE	LEAF ATTACHMENT
Spike	**Irregular**	**Simple**	**Opposite**

Dwarf Violet Iris

Iris verna

Family: Iris (Iridaceae)

Height: 2–6" (5–15 cm)

Flower: deep purple to lavender, 2½" (6 cm) wide, of 3 spreading drooping sepals and 3 erect petals that curve inward; each sepal has hairy orange center stripe on deep purple-veined white throat; each petal solid-colored; 1–2 flowers on single short stalk

Leaf: flat, lance-shaped, 4" (10 cm) long, brilliant green, basally attached or clasping the single stalk; 5–9 leaves tower over the flower

Fruit: green capsule, turning brown, 1" (2.5 cm) long, with 3 angles

Bloom: spring, summer

Cycle/Origin: perennial; native

Habitat: pinewoods, swamp edges, sun to partial shade

Range: throughout North Carolina and northern and central South Carolina

Notes: When blooming, Dwarf Violet Iris is one of the shortest plants of all of the other species of iris found in the Carolinas. Its purple blossoms are strongly fragrant. Range overlaps in the western half of North Carolina and northern South Carolina with the less fragrant Dwarf Crested Iris *(I. cristata)* (not shown), which has shorter and wider leaves than those of Dwarf Violet Iris and two hairy, crested ridges on the white base of the sepals.

FLOWER TYPE	LEAF TYPE	LEAF ATTACHMENT	LEAF ATTACHMENT	FRUIT
Irregular	**Simple**	**Basal**	**Clasping**	**Pod**

Texas Toadflax
Nuttallanthus texanus

Family: Snapdragon (Scrophulariaceae)

Height: 4–24" (10–61 cm)

Flower: loose spike cluster, 2½" (6 cm) long, of 10–12 pale lavender flowers; each flower, ½" (1 cm) long, 2-lobed erect upper lip; 3-lobed horizontal lower lip; conspicuous downward-curving spur; short stalk

Leaf: slender, ⅛–1" (.3–2.5 cm) long, smooth margin, stalkless; leaves alternately attached to erect stalk; slightly broader leaves are oppositely attached or whorled (forming a rosette) on the long prostrate stems at base of stalk

Bloom: spring, summer

Cycle/Origin: annual, biennial; native

Habitat: dry soils, cliffs, disturbed sites, grassy pinewoods

Range: throughout the Carolinas, except in the western-most mountainous counties of North Carolina

Notes: Toadflaxes are easily identified by their long spurs, which contain nectar that attracts pollinating insects, and are often referred to as spurred snapdragons. Canada Toadflax (pg. 137) is also widespread throughout the Carolinas, but it has smaller flowers and shorter spurs than Texas Toadflax blossoms. Often grows in abandoned fields with pink- or red-flowered Heartwing Sorrel (pg. 121), forming lavender and pinkish orange masses of flowers. Genus name is for Thomas Nuttall, premier naturalist of the early 1800s.

CLUSTER TYPE	FLOWER TYPE	LEAF TYPE	LEAF ATTACHMENT	LEAF ATTACHMENT
Spike	**Irregular**	**Simple**	**Alternate**	**Basal**

fruit

Winter Vetch

Vicia villosa

Family: Pea or Bean (Fabaceae)

Height: 12–36" (30–91 cm); vine

Flower: dense spike cluster, 3" (7.5 cm) long, of 10–40 drooping pea-like purple (rarely white) flowers; each tiny flower, ⅙–¼" (.4–.6 cm) long, 2-lipped; flowers grow along 1 side of spike

Leaf: compound, 5" (13 cm) long, composed of 5–10 pair of leaflets and a curling tendril at end of leaf; each thin oblong leaflet, ½–1" (1–2.5 cm) long, densely hairy; sprawling or climbing, angled hairy vine

Fruit: flattened pea-like green pod, 1" (2.5–3 cm) long, hairy, contains 2–8 seeds

Bloom: summer, fall

Cycle/Origin: annual, perennial, biennial; non-native

Habitat: disturbed areas, roadsides, old fields, sun

Range: throughout

Notes: A vine introduced from Europe that clings to other plants or structures with the tendrils at the ends of its compound leaves. Nutritious, it contains about 15 percent protein and is cultivated for hay in the U.S. Also used for soil improvement and erosion control. However, it is very invasive and has naturalized throughout much of the country. Easily recognized by its showy purple spikes and its stems and leaves, which are covered with long soft hairs and often appear grayish green. *Villosa* means "shaggy" or "woolly" in Latin.

CLUSTER TYPE	FLOWER TYPE	LEAF TYPE	LEAF ATTACHMENT	FRUIT
Spike	**Irregular**	**Compound**	**Alternate**	**Pod**

Thickleaf Phlox

Phlox carolina

Family: Phlox (Polemoniaceae)

Height: 3–4' (.9–1.2 m)

Flower: dense round cluster, 4" (10 cm) wide, of many purple flowers with yellow centers; each flower, ½–¾" (1–2 cm) wide, of 5 overlapping petals fused to form long narrow tube; petals can be dark pink, magenta or white; colored petals have lighter or darker streak at base forming a star around center

Leaf: oblong, 1½–5" (4–13 cm) long, thick, shiny, pointed tip, blunt base, stalkless; 5–12 pair of leaves; green-to-purplish stem; several stems per plant

Bloom: summer

Cycle/Origin: perennial; native

Habitat: dry to moist soils, edges of deciduous woods

Range: throughout South Carolina, western half of North Carolina

Notes: Also known as Carolina Phlox. Unlike most phlox leaves, which get progressively smaller going up the stem, Carolina Phlox leaves get gradually larger. Attractive, showy flower clusters atop tall erect stems make it a popular choice for flower gardens. Phlox are also good plants for butterfly gardens, as butterflies are attracted to the nectar. Seeded along highways by the North Carolina Department of Transportation.

CLUSTER TYPE	FLOWER TYPE	LEAF TYPE	LEAF ATTACHMENT
Round	**Regular**	**Simple**	**Opposite**

Eastern Smooth Beardtongue
Penstemon laevigatus

Family: Snapdragon (Scrophulariaceae)

Height: 12–36" (30–91 cm)

Flower: loose or dense spike cluster, 4–8" (10–20 cm) long, of pale purple, pink or white flowers; each flower, 1" (2.5 cm) long, petals fused into a tube, flaring widely at the mouth; 2-lobed erect upper and 3-lobed horizontal lower petals (lips); throat sometimes has dark purple or pink streaks

Leaf: basal, oval, 6–8" (15–20 cm) long, broadest above middle, small-toothed or smooth margin, on long stalks; stem leaf, lance-shaped, smaller, blunt base, pointed tip, mostly with smooth margin

Bloom: summer

Cycle/Origin: perennial; native

Habitat: clearings in rich woods, fallow fields, disturbed sites

Range: throughout the Carolinas, except in the western mountainous counties of North Carolina

Notes: There are more than 20 species of penstemon in the southeastern United States, many of which hybridize, making them difficult to identify. The brushy yellow tip ("beard") on the fifth stamen that is characteristic to beardtongues is not as obvious in this species. Eustis Lake Beardtongue (pg. 131) has a much narrower flower tube that does not flare as widely at the mouth.

CLUSTER TYPE	FLOWER TYPE	LEAF TYPE	LEAF ATTACHMENT	LEAF ATTACHMENT	LEAF ATTACHMENT
Spike	**Irregular**	**Simple**	**Opposite**	**Basal**	**Clasping**

fruit

Kudzu
Pueraria montana

Family: Pea or Bean (Fabaceae)

Height: 30–100' (9.1–30 m); vine

Flower: upright spike cluster, 4–8" (10–20 cm) long, of pea-like reddish purple flowers; each flower, 1" (2.5 cm) long; flowers smell like grapes

Leaf: compound, 6" (15 cm) long, made up of 3 leaflets; each wide leaflet, 4–6" (10–15 cm) long, smooth edged or deeply divided into 2–3 lobes, on long stalks; on trailing, climbing, semi-woody vine

Fruit: bean-like green pod, turning brown, 3¼" (8 cm) long, wavy, fuzzy edges, contains 3–10 seeds

Bloom: summer, fall

Cycle/Origin: perennial; non-native

Habitat: forest edges, old fields, woods, disturbed sites, sun

Range: throughout

Notes: Introduced from Japan as a forage crop that could also be used to control soil erosion. Kudzu has become a noxious weed, overgrowing trees and other plants, shading and choking them out. Spreads by runners (rarely sets seed in the Carolinas) and can grow as much as a foot per day. The leaves are frost sensitive, but digging it out to eradicate it is a difficult task due to its long taproot, which can weigh up to 400 pounds (180 kg) and grow as long as 6 feet (1.8 m). Native vines such as Trumpet Creeper (pg. 215) and Purple Passionflower (pg. 169) are better choices for cultivation.

CLUSTER TYPE	FLOWER TYPE	LEAF TYPE	LEAF ATTACHMENT	FRUIT
Spike	**Irregular**	**Compound**	**Alternate**	**Pod**

Downy Lobelia
Lobelia puberula

Family: Bellflower (Campanulaceae)

Height: 1–4' (30–122 cm)

Flower: spike cluster, 4–12" (10–30 cm) long, of lavender-to-blue flowers with white centers; each flower, 1" (2.5 cm) long, hairy, oval petals (lips) fused into a tube; upper 2 lips much smaller and stick up like a donkey's ears; 2 of lower 3 horizontal lips have white bases; flowers attach along 1 side of stalk

Leaf: oval (upper) or teardrop-shaped (lower), 2–4" (5–10 cm) long, wrinkled, covered with soft hairs above, pointed tip, small teeth widely spaced along margin, stalkless

Bloom: summer, fall

Cycle/Origin: perennial; native

Habitat: wet to fairly dry sandy soils, open woods, mountain bogs, swamps, wet meadows, forest edges

Range: throughout

Notes: "Downy" in the common name is apt for this lobelia, as it can be distinguished from all the other purple- or blue-flowered lobelias in the Carolinas by the short hairs covering its flowers, leaves and stems. Sometimes called Blue Cardinal Flower since it resembles Cardinal Flower (pg. 217), a relative with red flowers that is often found in the same areas. Available at local garden centers, this plant is a good choice for gardens with shady moist spots.

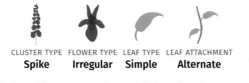

CLUSTER TYPE **Spike**   FLOWER TYPE **Irregular**   LEAF TYPE **Simple**   LEAF ATTACHMENT **Alternate**

Lyreleaf Sage

Salvia lyrata

Family: Mint (Lamiaceae)

Height: 12–24" (30–61 cm)

Flower: spike cluster, 4–12" (10–30 cm) long, of whorls of 4–8 pale lavender-to-deep blue flowers; each flower, 1" (2.5 cm) long, petals fuse to form long tube (corolla), arched upper lip, 2-lobed lower lip longer than upper; pointed maroon calyx cups the flower

Leaf: basal, lyre-shaped, 3–8" (7.5–20 cm) long, deeply and symmetrically lobed, veins outlined in maroon, sparsely haired reddish leafstalk; few (or absent) elliptical smaller stem leaves; 4-sided hairy stem

Fruit: reddish brown pod, open cup-shaped; contains dimpled, dark brown nutlets

Bloom: spring, summer

Cycle/Origin: perennial; native

Habitat: fields, open woods, thickets, roadsides, creek banks

Range: throughout

Notes: The flower clusters are whorled around and widely spaced along a single hairy stem. A tough, useful plant that can be sown in wildflower meadows. Good for borders and lawns as it tolerates mowing, but it can become weedy and invasive. The color of the flowers intensifies with more shade. Young leaves taste minty and can be eaten in salads. Dried plant parts are used to brew a tea that was once used to treat asthma, colds or other respiratory ailments.

CLUSTER TYPE	FLOWER TYPE	LEAF TYPE	LEAF ATTACHMENT	FRUIT
Spike	**Irregular**	**Simple Lobed**	**Basal**	**Pod**

New York Ironweed
Vernonia noveboracensis

Family: Aster (Asteraceae)

Height: 3–7' (.9–2.1 m)

Flower: loose irregular flat cluster, 3–5" (7.5–13 cm) wide, of 30–55 purple flower heads; each flower head, ½–¾" (1–2 cm) wide, of tiny tubular disk flowers only

Leaf: narrowly lance-shaped, 4–12" (10–30 cm) long, sharply small-toothed margin, pointed tip, smooth above, soft white hairs below; many leaves on smooth to slightly hairy, green-to-purplish stem

Bloom: summer, fall

Cycle/Origin: perennial; native

Habitat: moist to wet soils, woods, marshes, stream edges, thickets, meadows, low areas, sun to partial shade

Range: throughout

Notes: "Iron" refers to the rust-colored dried flower heads and reddish seeds, which resemble the color of rusted iron. Cherokee Indians used ironweed root to make a tea to relieve menstrual cramps. A tall plant that looks attractive planted behind other flowers in gardens and a good choice for butterfly gardens. Readily self-seeds, so remove the faded flower heads if you don't want it to spread. Differs from some other ironweeds as it lacks a basal rosette of leaves. Found in southeastern North Carolina and eastern South Carolina, the similar Tall Ironweed (*V. angustifolia*) (not shown) has much narrower, oppositely attached leaves and has hairy stems.

CLUSTER TYPE **Flat** FLOWER TYPE **Composite** LEAF TYPE **Simple** LEAF ATTACHMENT **Alternate**

Venus' Pride

Houstonia purpurea

Family: Madder (Rubiaceae)

Height: 6–20" (15–50 cm)

Flower: flat cluster, 5" (13 cm) wide, of 3–11 light purple-to-white flowers streaked with lavender (rarely all deep purple); each tubular flower, ½" (1 cm) long, made up of 4 pointed petals fused together to form a tube, then flaring out

Leaf: heart-shaped or oblong and lance-shaped, ½–2" (1–5 cm) long, 3-5 veins, stalkless; numerous opposite pairs attach to the several branching stems

Bloom: spring, summer

Cycle/Origin: perennial; native

Habitat: moist to dry soils, woods, pine forests, near rocky outcroppings, stream banks, along roads, sun to partial shade

Range: western two-thirds of the Carolinas

Notes: This species has three recognized varieties, which all differ quite a bit from each other in flower color and shape of the leaves. However, Venus' Pride can always be identified by the 3–5 visible veins on the leaves and the location (at the top of the stems) of its purple-to-white flowers. Range overlaps with the much shorter Azure Bluet (pg. 21), which has smaller and fewer leaves. The genus name *Houstonia* is for Scottish physician and botanist Dr. William Houston, who collected and wrote about plants in the 1700s.

CLUSTER TYPE	FLOWER TYPE	LEAF TYPE	LEAF ATTACHMENT
Flat	**Tube**	**Simple**	**Opposite**

Shaggy Blazing Star
Liatris pilosa

Family: Aster (Asteraceae)

Height: 3–5' (.9–1.5 m)

Flower: spike cluster, 6–8" (15–20 cm) long, of shaggy reddish purple flower heads; each flower head, ½–¾" (1–2 cm) wide, of 7–14 densely packed, tubular, star-shaped florets (disk flowers) with spiky flower parts protruding from each floret; each floret made of 5 flared petals with pointed lobes

Leaf: thin, grass-like, 2–8" (5–20 cm) long, with long white hairs on margin near the base; leaves get shorter farther up the rough stem

Bloom: fall

Cycle/Origin: perennial; native

Habitat: moist to dry, rocky or sandy soils, burned clearings, sandhills, open pinewoods, roadsides, old fields

Range: throughout

Notes: Shaggy Blazing Star has a spike cluster of ragged reddish purple flowers. Its many grass-like leaves alternate about every inch along the stem, with the upper leaves getting progressively shorter. Species name *pilosa* is Latin for "hairy" and refers to the hairs inside the tubular disk flowers. It is difficult to distinguish among species of blazing star. The very similar Dense Blazing Star (*L. spicata*) (not shown) is frequently cultivated and is planted along highways by the North Carolina Department of Transportation.

| CLUSTER TYPE | FLOWER TYPE | LEAF TYPE | LEAF ATTACHMENT |
| **Spike** | **Composite** | **Simple** | **Alternate** |

Red Clover

Trifolium pratense

Family: Pea or Bean (Fabaceae)

Height: 6–24" (15–61 cm)

Flower: round cluster, 1" (2.5 cm) wide, of 50–100 rosy red flowers; each flower, ⅛–¼" (.3–.6 cm) long; appears as 1 large red flower

Leaf: typical clover leaf, ½–2" (1–5 cm) wide, made up of 3 leaflets; each leaflet has white markings in a V shape (chevron), upper leaves stalkless, lower leaves on stalks

Bloom: spring, summer, fall

Cycle/Origin: perennial, biennial; non-native

Habitat: wet or dry soils, disturbed areas, old fields, pastures, sun

Range: throughout

Notes: A native of Europe, Red Clover was introduced to North America as a hay and pasture crop. It has since escaped to the wild and is now one of the most common roadside plants. Still grown as a rotation crop to improve soil fertility because its roots fix nitrogen into the soil. Genus name *Trifolium* means "three leaves," which describes the three leaflets, while species name *pratense* means "meadows" or "of the fields," where it grows. Pollinated nearly exclusively by honeybees. Without these insects, it is unable to produce seeds and will eventually die out. Seeds can lay dormant for years before sprouting.

CLUSTER TYPE
Round

FLOWER TYPE
Irregular

LEAF TYPE
Compound

LEAF ATTACHMENT
Alternate

Fire Pink

Silene virginica

Family: Pink (Caryophyllaceae)

Height: 12–24" (30–61 cm)

Flower: bright red, 1½" (4 cm) wide, made of 5 deeply notched, narrow petals; several flowers on stalks from upper leaf junctions

Leaf: basal, oblong or spoon-shaped, 2–6" (5–15 cm) long, 2–4 pair of narrow lance-shaped stem leaves, directly attached to sticky hairy stem

Bloom: late spring, early summer

Cycle/Origin: perennial; native

Habitat: rich open woodlands, rocky outcroppings, cracks in cliffs, riverbanks, grassy woodland borders

Range: western two-thirds of the Carolinas

Notes: Fire Pink is a short-lived wildflower that is most common in the hills and mountains of the Carolinas and rarely is found along the coast. One of nearly 20 species in the genus *Silene*, most of which are found in the Carolinas. This native and two non-native relatives, Sweet William (*S. armeria*) and Nodding Catchfly (*S. pendula*) (neither shown), have been planted along highways in North Carolina. Also called Catchfly, referring to the insects getting caught by the sticky sap that the hairs on the stems exude. "Pink" refers to the Pink family of plants and not the color of the flowers, which are bright red and attract hummingbirds. Reproduces mostly from seeds, often forming impressive masses of blooming plants.

FLOWER TYPE **Regular**   LEAF TYPE **Simple**   LEAF ATTACHMENT **Opposite**   LEAF ATTACHMENT **Basal**

Scarlet Beebalm
Monarda didyma

Family: Mint (Lamiaceae)

Height: 2–5' (61–152 cm)

Flower: round cluster, 1½" (4 cm) wide, of more than 30 deep scarlet flowers; each flower, ½" (1 cm) long, made up of 2 petals (lips); upper smaller than 3-lobed, ragged-tipped lower lip; long protruding flower parts; red bracts below flower cluster

Leaf: lance-shaped, 3–6" (7–15 cm) long, dull green, coarse-toothed margin, pointed tip, minty scent; oppositely attached; each pair of leaves rotated at right angles to next pair; fuzzy square stem

Bloom: summer, fall

Cycle/Origin: perennial; native, non-native

Habitat: slope seepages, stream banks, woods, boggy areas

Range: westernmost counties of North Carolina, scattered locations in South Carolina

Notes: This plant is seeded along highways in North Carolina. Non-native to South Carolina and rarely escaping to the wild, it is often cultivated in gardens throughout the state to attract hummingbirds. The flower is not fragrant, but butterflies and bees also love the nectar of this bloom. Leaves and stems emit a strong minty odor when crushed. Also called Oswego Tea because Oswego Indians of New York used its leaves for a tea to treat indigestion. Younger leaves and petals are eaten in salads or are used to season fried potatoes.

CLUSTER TYPE	FLOWER TYPE	LEAF TYPE	LEAF ATTACHMENT
Round	**Irregular**	**Simple**	**Opposite**

flower

Bull Thistle
Cirsium vulgare

Family: Aster (Asteraceae)

Height: 2–6' (.6–1.8 m)

Flower: reddish purple, 1½–2" (4–5 cm) wide, large flower head made up of thin tubular disk flowers; sits on a wide spiny green base that narrows near its center; 1 to several flower heads per stem

Leaf: narrowly elliptical, 3–6" (7.5–15 cm) long, with many lobes; each lobe ends in a sharp spine; spines and hairs on stems and undersides of leaves

Bloom: summer, fall

Cycle/Origin: biennial; non-native

Habitat: dry or disturbed soils, open fields, roadsides, along railroads, sun

Range: western half of the Carolinas

Notes: The spiniest of many different thistle species found in the Carolinas. However, Horrid Thistle (pg. 173) rivals it for the honor. Bull Thistle is a true biennial, producing a low rosette of leaves its first year and sending up a tall flower stalk in the second. A favorite flower of large bees and butterflies, Bull Thistle's little seeds are attached to tiny parachute-like thistledown that carry them away on the wind after pollination. The seeds are a preferred food for American Goldfinches, which also use the thistledown to line their nests, thus they wait until thistles bloom in late summer to raise their young. A common invader of disturbed sites.

FLOWER TYPE
Irregular

LEAF TYPE
Simple Lobed

LEAF ATTACHMENT
Alternate

Little Sweet Betsy

Trillium cuneatum

Family: Lily (Liliaceae)

Height: 8–16" (20–40 cm)

Flower: dull or brownish red (sometimes green or yellow), 1½–3" (4–7.5 cm) long, 3 erect elliptical petals and 3 horizontal lance-shaped sepals; petals and sepals have bluntly pointed tips; fruity fragrance

Leaf: broadly oval, 3–7" (7.5–18 cm) long, mottled gray-green on light green, whorl of 3 leaves

Fruit: cylindrical green berry, turning maroon when ripe, ½" (1 cm) long

Bloom: spring, summer

Cycle/Origin: perennial; native

Habitat: moist soils, cove forests, shade

Range: western half of the Carolinas

Notes: "Little" is a misnomer, as this is a medium-sized trillium. Also called Purple Toadshade for the broad mottled leaves, which resemble the skin of a toad and may provide shade for the amphibian. Sometimes abundant during spring in cove forests, which are rich deciduous woods sheltered by the dip of land surrounding a stream. Range overlaps in South Carolina with Spotted Wakerobin *(T. maculatum)* and Yellow Wakerobin *(T. luteum)* (neither shown). Difficult to distinguish from Spotted Wakerobin, which has erect or downward-curving sepals. Yellow Wakerobin is also similar, but its leaves are more mottled and its yellow flowers smell like citrus fruit.

FLOWER TYPE	LEAF TYPE	LEAF ATTACHMENT	FRUIT
Regular	**Simple**	**Whorl**	**Berry**

fruit

Red Columbine
Aquilegia canadensis

Family: Buttercup (Ranunculaceae)

Height: 1–4' (30–122 cm)

Flower: orangish red and yellow, 1–2" (2.5–5 cm) long, group of 5 upside-down tubes form a yellow-tipped bell containing nectar-filled spurs

Leaf: compound, 4–6" (10–15 cm) long, made up of 9–27 thin light green leaflets; each leaflet has 3 bluntly toothed lobes; leaves on long leafstalks

Fruit: pod-like green container, turning brown and papery at maturity; 1¼" (3 cm) long, has shiny round seeds

Bloom: spring, summer

Cycle/Origin: perennial; native

Habitat: rocky places, open deciduous woods, partial shade

Range: scattered throughout North Carolina, a few north-western counties in South Carolina

Notes: The only native columbine in the Carolinas. A cultivated columbine will sometimes escape into the wild. Children often mistake Columbine for honeysuckle and bite off its long spurs to suck out the nectar. Its nectar tubes make it a favorite flower of hummingbirds and long-tongued moths. Some insects chew holes in its tubes, cheating to get a little nectar. Once considered for our national wildflower because its flower resembles the talons of the Bald Eagle. Grows well in gardens, but please don't dig up from the wild—plant only seeds.

FLOWER TYPE	LEAF TYPE	LEAF ATTACHMENT	FRUIT
Bell	**Compound**	**Alternate**	**Pod**

Trumpet Honeysuckle
Lonicera sempervirens

Family: Honeysuckle (Caprifoliaceae)

Height: 15–25' (4.6–7.6 m); vine

Flower: deep rosy red outside with orange or yellow inside, 1–2" (2.5–5 cm) long, 5 petals fused to form slender tube, flaring abruptly at top; in groups of 6 flowers

Leaf: broadly oval, 1–3" (2.5–7.5 cm) long, evergreen, slightly curving downward at edges, sometimes hairy above; each pair of leaves rotated at right angles to next pair, final pair perfoliate

Fruit: round green berry, turning orangish red when ripe, ¼" (.6 cm) wide, pulpy, slightly translucent

Bloom: spring, summer

Cycle/Origin: perennial; native

Habitat: open woods, thickets, disturbed sites, forest edges

Range: throughout, except in the westernmost mountainous counties of North Carolina

Notes: Not invasive like its exotic relative Japanese Honeysuckle (pg. 263), this woody vine is a better choice for cultivation as it won't strangle the tree or shrub upon which it grows. Grows a multitude of showy flowers per vine if in full sun. Sometimes will flower again in the fall. Although its flowers are not fragrant, the nectar attracts hummingbirds and butterflies; other birds eat the fruit. Cultivated varieties are available with orange, yellow or pink flowers. Can be a trailing, climbing or counterclockwise-twining vine.

FLOWER TYPE	LEAF TYPE	LEAF ATTACHMENT	LEAF ATTACHMENT	FRUIT
Tube	**Simple**	**Opposite**	**Perfoliate**	**Berry**

Woodland Pinkroot

Spigelia marilandica

Family: Logania (Loganiaceae)

Height: 12–24" (30–61 cm)

Flower: curving spike cluster, 4" (10 cm) long, of deep red flowers outside with yellow inside; each narrow flower, 1–2½" (2.5–6 cm) long, flares outward into a star shape; flowers on only 1 side of flower stalk

Leaf: teardrop-shaped, 2–4½" (5–11 cm) long, glossy dark green, smooth margin, stalkless; 4–7 pair of leaves; slightly winged, smooth squarish stem

Fruit: spherical green pod, turning black, ¼–⅓" (.6–.8 cm) wide; explodes (making a firecracker-like sound) at maturity and disperses the seeds

Bloom: summer

Cycle/Origin: perennial; native

Habitat: shaded or open woods, forest edges, stream banks

Range: throughout South Carolina, southwestern North Carolina

Notes: A favorite of Ruby-throated Hummingbirds. Tolerates cultivation in shady parts of the garden, where most flowers that attract hummingbirds won't grow. Flowers at the bottom of the spike open first. Keep the plant blooming longer by plucking off the withered blooms. Left alone, the plant will self-seed and form a small colony, so you may wish to divide the root ball before the plant sprouts in the spring. Be careful—the root contains a poisonous alkaloid.

CLUSTER TYPE	FLOWER TYPE	LEAF TYPE	LEAF ATTACHMENT	FRUIT
Spike	**Tube**	**Simple**	**Opposite**	**Pod**

213

fruit

Trumpet Creeper
Campsis radicans

Family: Trumpet Creeper (Bignoniaceae)

Height: 20–30' (6.1–9.1 m); vine

Flower: round cluster, 4–15" (10–38 cm) wide, of 2–10 deep red or orangish red flowers; each flower, 3" (7.5 cm) long, 5 petals fused to form a trumpet shape; fused yellow sepals (calyx) at base of flower look like an inverted crown

Leaf: compound, 6–15" (15–38 cm) long, stalked, made up of 7–15 leaflets; each leaflet, 1–4" (2.5–10 cm) long, dark green, coarsely toothed, pointed tip

Fruit: crescent-shaped green pod, turning tannish brown, 6" (15 cm) long, beaked, flattened, woody, contains winged seeds

Bloom: summer

Cycle/Origin: perennial; native

Habitat: dry soils, disturbed areas, forest edges, thickets, sun

Range: throughout

Notes: This showy vine is cultivated, but is aggressive and can be extremely invasive, especially in the South. Green or woody stems climb by growing aerial roots that cling with a strong adhesive, making it very difficult to detach the vine from any structure. Ants live inside the flowers, feeding on small nectar glands and possibly deterring animals from eating the newly forming seed-pods. Some people develop a rash after contact with the leaves or flowers.

CLUSTER TYPE
Round

FLOWER TYPE
Tube

LEAF TYPE
Compound

LEAF ATTACHMENT
Opposite

FRUIT
Pod

Cardinal Flower

Lobelia cardinalis

Family: Bellflower (Campanulaceae)

Height: 2–4' (61–122 cm)

Flower: tall open spike cluster, 12–24" (30–61 cm) long, of scarlet red flowers; each flower, 1½" (4 cm) wide, 5 narrow petals (2 upper and 3 spreading lower) unite to form a thin tube at its base; flowers alternate on stem; lower flowers open before upper flowers

Leaf: thin, lance-shaped, 2–6" (5–15 cm) long, toothed margin, pointed tip; purplish green stem contains a milky sap

Bloom: summer, fall

Cycle/Origin: perennial; native

Habitat: wet soils, along wetlands, meadows, partial shade

Range: throughout

Notes: By far one of the most spectacular wildflowers of the Carolinas, Cardinal Flower is found growing in small patches along streams and rivers. Can be grown in gardens, but its roots need to be wet and its flowers must have some sunlight. Please do not dig this plant from the wild—it can be purchased at garden centers. Not very successful at reproducing, perhaps because it can be pollinated only by hummingbirds. "Cardinal" in the common name refers to Roman Catholic cardinals, whose bright red robes resemble the scarlet red color of the flowers. Occasionally produces white or rose-colored blooms. All parts of the plant are poisonous.

CLUSTER TYPE	FLOWER TYPE	LEAF TYPE	LEAF ATTACHMENT
Spike	**Irregular**	**Simple**	**Alternate**

Sericea Lespedeza

Lespedeza cuneata

Family: Pea or Bean (Fabaceae)

Height: 3–7' (.9–2.1 m)

Flower: white or cream, ¼" (.6 cm) long, pea-like, purple throat, upper petal has pinkish purple veins; 1–4 flowers in a cluster at upper leaf attachment (axis)

Leaf: compound, made up of 3 oblong leaflets; each leaflet, 1" (2.5 cm) long, green above, grayish green below; stalked lower leaves, stalkless upper leaves

Bloom: summer, fall

Cycle/Origin: perennial; non-native

Habitat: dry or moist soils, disturbed areas, marshes, sun

Range: throughout

Notes: Originally introduced from Asia and Australia in the 1800s as a hardy plant that can grow in poor soils, intended to control erosion along roads and as forage for cattle. However, the tannins in older leaves make it unpalatable to cows. Now considered invasive, some recommend it no longer be planted for any purpose. Grows slowly, but once established, its deep roots and tough stems make it hard to eradicate. Interestingly, several other lespedeza species in the Carolinas have pink blooms rather than the white flowers of this plant.

FLOWER TYPE
Irregular

LEAF TYPE
Compound

LEAF ATTACHMENT
Alternate

Common Chickweed

Stellaria media

Family: Pink (Caryophyllaceae)

Height: 3–9" (7.5–23 cm)

Flower: white, ¼" (.6 cm) wide, star-shaped, made up of 5 deeply divided petals (each appearing like 2 oblong petals) that make the flower look as if it has 10 petals; flowers found singly at ends of tiny stalks

Leaf: oval, ½–1" (1–2.5 cm) long, dark green or pale yellowish green, pointed tip, toothless; upper leaves clasp the stem, lower leaves attach by short thin stalks often covered with tiny hairs; single line of long white hairs along 1 side of reddish green stem

Bloom: spring, summer, fall

Cycle/Origin: annual, perennial; non-native

Habitat: wet or dry soils, disturbed areas, meadows, lawns

Range: throughout

Notes: A common weak-stemmed plant that lies across the ground in large mats, displaying many flowers per plant. Trailing stems can grow as long as 20 inches (50 cm). When its white flowers are open, they look like many tiny stars. Gardeners are often pestered by the prodigious growth of this plant, which is easily pulled out of the ground. One of several species of chickweed in the Carolinas. Has round-tipped petals, unlike Star Chickweed (*S. pubera*) (not shown), which has long petals with pointed tips.

FLOWER TYPE **Regular**   LEAF TYPE **Simple**   LEAF ATTACHMENT **Opposite**

Carolina Geranium
Geranium carolinianum

Family: Geranium (Geraniaceae)

Height: 6–20" (15–50 cm)

Flower: white to pinkish, ½" (1 cm) wide, made up of 5 veined notched petals; hairy pointed green bracts cup the flower; flowers occur singly or in pairs

Leaf: oval to nearly round, lobed, 3" (7.5 cm) wide, divided into 3–7 deep lobes as wide as they are long; each lobe in turn divided into lobes with toothed margins; on long leafstalk

Fruit: narrow pointed green capsule, turning brown, 1" (2.5 cm) long, shaped like a crane's bill; splits open when ripe, peeling back to show black seeds at base of "beak"

Bloom: summer

Cycle/Origin: annual, biennial; native

Habitat: dry or sandy soils, fields, meadows, roadsides, sun

Range: throughout

Notes: A showy, but weedy plant commonly found wherever the soil has been disturbed. Unlike the shade-loving Spotted Geranium (pg. 153), it prefers to grow in sunny spots. This species and Wild Geranium share another common name, Carolina Crane's Bill, named for the peculiar shape of its seed capsule. Surprisingly, the common houseplant geranium is not in the *Geranium* genus, but actually is a member of the South African genus *Pelargonium*.

FLOWER TYPE
Regular

LEAF TYPE
Simple Lobed

LEAF ATTACHMENT
Alternate

FRUIT
Pod

Striped Prince's Pine
Chimaphila maculata

Family: Wintergreen (Pyrolaceae)

Height: 4–8" (10–20 cm)

Flower: white to pinkish, ½" (1 cm) wide, 5 petals pointing upward, green-and-white centers protruding below the rest of flower; up to 5 flowers droop from long orange stalk rising from reddish violet stem

Leaf: lance-shaped, 1–3" (2.5–7.5 cm) long, green with prominent white veins, thick, waxy, widely spaced sharp teeth; 1–3 leaves are oppositely, whorled or alternately attached at the base of stem and sometimes midway up; evergreen, turning dark purplish green in winter

Fruit: greenish yellow capsule, turning orangish brown, ¼" (.6 cm) wide, spherical and dimpled (looks like a squashed beach ball), attached to upright stalk

Bloom: summer

Cycle/Origin: perennial; native

Habitat: moist soils, upland woods, pine forests, oak-hickory forests, shade

Range: throughout

Notes: Used medicinally prior to the invention of antibiotics, the plant has compounds now proven to have anti-bacterial properties. However, some people do develop a rash after touching the leaves. Sometimes used in flavoring candy and beer. Also called Pipsissewa.

FLOWER TYPE **Regular**   LEAF TYPE **Simple**   LEAF ATTACHMENT **Whorl**   FRUIT **Pod**

Hairy White Oldfield Aster
Symphyotrichum pilosum

Family: Aster (Asteraceae)

Height: 2–5' (61–152 cm)

Flower: white (sometimes pink or pale purple) flower head, ½–¾" (1–2 cm) wide, made up of 16–35 petals (ray flowers) surrounding a bright yellow center (disk flowers); center turns reddish when pollinated; 40–100 flower heads on diffusely branching stems

Leaf: basal, spoon-shaped, 1–4" (2.5–10 cm) long, long leafstalk; upper leaves smaller, narrower, stalkless; both types smooth edged or slightly toothed; leaves and multi-branched stem densely or sparingly hairy with long soft white hairs

Bloom: late summer, fall

Cycle/Origin: perennial; native

Habitat: disturbed ground, old fields, sun to partial shade

Range: throughout

Notes: The basal and lower stem leaves of this aster drop off before the flowers bloom, leaving the lower stem nearly leafless. This is one of most common of the more than 30 species of aster in the southeastern United States. Seeded along with other related asters along North Carolina highways. When its flowers are white, the usually lavender-flowered Rice Button Aster (pg. 141) is a look-alike of this species. Serves as a larval host for the Pearl Crescent butterfly.

FLOWER TYPE **Composite** LEAF TYPE **Simple** LEAF ATTACHMENT **Alternate** LEAF ATTACHMENT **Basal**

Primroseleaf Violet
Viola primulifolia

Family: Violet (Violaceae)

Height: 4–6" (10–15 cm)

Flower: white, ½–¾" (1–2 cm) wide, 2 upper petals folded backward, lower middle petal with purplish veins toward base, lower 2 side petals white (sometimes yellow) at base; yellowish red center; each flower usually above leaves on own short stalk

Leaf: basal, oval or heart-shaped, 1–2½" (2.5–6 cm) long, smooth or hairy, blunt-toothed margin, on broadly winged reddish stalk; plant is stemless until flowering, then develops runners

Fruit: elliptical green capsule, ⅜" (.9 cm) long, contains reddish brown seeds

Bloom: spring, summer

Cycle/Origin: annual; native

Habitat: moist to wet sandy soils, bogs, stream edges, pond banks, open meadows, wet woods, sun to shade

Range: throughout

Notes: Once considered a separate species, the Primroseleaf Violet is now thought to be a common hybrid between Bog White Violet *(V. lanceolata)* and Small White Violet *(V. macloskeyi)* (neither shown). Especially common in the eastern half of the Carolinas. The species name is from Latin words combined to mean "primrose leaf" and refer to the leaves, which resemble those of primroses.

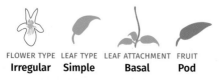

FLOWER TYPE **Irregular**   LEAF TYPE **Simple**   LEAF ATTACHMENT **Basal**   FRUIT **Pod**

single

Indian Pipe
Monotropa uniflora

Family: Indian Pipe (Monotropaceae)

Height: 3–9" (7.5–23 cm)

Flower: white (sometimes pink), ½–1" (1–2.5 cm) long, made up of 4–5 waxy petals fused together; bell-shaped flower hangs from end of a white stem; 1 bell flower per plant

Leaf: very small and scale-like, ¼" (.6 cm) long; often goes unnoticed

Fruit: oval pod-like white capsule, turning black, ¼–½" (.6–1 cm) long

Bloom: summer, fall

Cycle/Origin: perennial; native

Habitat: moist rich soils, woods, shade

Range: throughout

Notes: A unique plant of the forest, Indian Pipe lacks chlorophyll, so it appears white. Turns pink after fertilization and becomes black with age or if picked. Does not make food for itself like other plants, instead getting nourishment from dead or decaying plant material (saprophytic) through a mutually beneficial fungal relationship (mycorrhiza). Some believe it is a parasitic plant, living off other living plants, killing its hosts. Often grows in small clumps, but can grow alone (see inset). Species name means "one flower," describing its one bell flower per plant. Flower turns upright after pollination, an action described by genus name *Monotropa,* meaning "one turn."

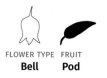

FLOWER TYPE FRUIT
Bell **Pod**

New Jersey Tea
Ceanothus americanus

Family: Buckthorn (Rhamnaceae)

Height: 8–36" (20–91 cm); shrub

Flower: semi-cylindrical round-tipped spike cluster, ½–1½" (1–4 cm) long, of tiny white flowers; each flower, ⅙" (.4 cm) wide, made up of 5 petals; part of each petal folding inward toward center, part spreading outward and shaped like a claw; several clusters per plant top the branching stem

Leaf: oval, 2–4" (5–10 cm) long, dark green, wrinkled above, pointed tip, blunt-toothed margin; leaves alternate along hairy stem

Fruit: thinly fleshed green capsule, turning deep blackish purple, ¼" (.6 cm) wide, 3-parted

Bloom: summer

Cycle/Origin: perennial; native

Habitat: dry sandy soils, open upland woods, rocky hills, forest edges, roadsides, sun

Range: throughout

Notes: Named because the early American colonists dried and boiled the leaves to make tea when oriental black tea was too expensive due to British taxes and an embargo. Unlike black tea, it does not contain caffeine. The root contains compounds that lower blood pressure, and the leaves and roots were used medicinally by American Indians. This small shrub springs back readily after a fire.

CLUSTER TYPE	FLOWER TYPE	LEAF TYPE	LEAF ATTACHMENT	FRUIT
Spike	**Regular**	**Simple**	**Alternate**	**Pod**

fruit

Partridgeberry
Mitchella repens

Family: Madder (Rubiaceae)

Height: 4–12" (10–30 cm)

Flower: white, ¾" (2 cm) long, 3–6 (usually 4) petals fused into tube and flaring outward into points, many white hairs on upper surface; flowers occur in pairs, united at base by sepals (calyx)

Leaf: oval, ½–1" (1–2.5 cm) long, evergreen, dark green with whitish central vein above, yellowish green below, leathery, smooth margin; low creeping stem

Fruit: 2-dimpled spherical red berry, ¼" (.6 cm) wide

Bloom: summer

Cycle/Origin: perennial; native

Habitat: moist sandy soils, stream banks, bogs, rich woods, edges of sandstone cliffs, full to partial shade

Range: throughout

Notes: The Partridgeberry is a low-growing, shade-loving ground cover that forms attractive mats of dark green vegetation. Its pairs of fragrant white flowers are small and not very showy, but after fertilization, the female plant parts of each pair fuse together and result in a single dimpled red berry that stands out against the forest floor. Evergreen, it tolerates cold winters. The plant was used medicinally as recently as the early 1900s to prepare women for childbirth, as well as to ease menstrual cramps. The edible berry (relished by birds) is still used as a homeopathic remedy.

FLOWER TYPE
Tube

LEAF TYPE
Simple

LEAF ATTACHMENT
Opposite

FRUIT
Berry

Rue Anemone
Thalictrum thalictroides

Family: Buttercup (Ranunculaceae)

Height: 4–8" (10–20 cm)

Flower: white to pink to lavender, 1" (2.5 cm) wide, made up of 5–10 petal-like sepals and a green center; 2–3 flowers per plant

Leaf: leaves appear to be simple lobed, but are actually 5–8 compound leaves, each composed of 3 leaflets, 1" (2.5 cm) long; each leaflet has 3 rounded tips; leaves whorled just below the flowers

Bloom: early spring

Cycle/Origin: perennial; native

Habitat: wet soils, deciduous woods, partial sun

Range: western two-thirds of the Carolinas

Notes: A woodland bloomer of early spring, Rue Anemone usually grows in large groups, carpeting the forest floor. At a height of 3–4 inches (7.5–10 cm) from the ground, its single stem branches into several leafstalks and flower stalks. Each plant has two or three flowers, with one flower per stalk. Flower color ranges widely from white to pink to lavender. The flowers lack nectar, instead attracting insects by their color and shape. It reproduces mainly by underground stems (rhizomes). This plant somewhat resembles plants in the genera *Hepatica* and *Anemone* and was once classified as a member of the latter genus, as its leaves are similar to anemone leaves.

FLOWER TYPE
Regular

LEAF TYPE
Compound

LEAF ATTACHMENT
Whorl

237

Tall Thimbleweed

Anemone virginiana

Family: Buttercup (Ranunculaceae)

Height: 24–36" (61–91 cm)

Flower: thimble-shaped green center, 1" (2.5 cm) tall and ½" (1 cm) wide, surrounded by 5 greenish white sepals (often mistaken for petals), ¾" (2 cm) long; sepals are slightly cupped with hairy underside; 2–3 flowers on a single long thin stalk

Leaf: basal, lobed, 3" (7.5 cm) long, divided into 3 coarsely toothed lobes; upper stem leaves (cauline) are similar, but smaller and in whorls around stem

Fruit: thimble-shaped green capsule, turning white and cottony, 1¼" (3 cm) long, densely spiny

Bloom: summer

Cycle/Origin: perennial; native

Habitat: dry rich soils, rocky outcroppings, open woods, sun

Range: throughout North Carolina, western half of South Carolina

Notes: Also called Virginia Thimbleweed. One of several species of *Anemone* in the Carolinas, this is a single-stemmed plant that has two or three sets of whorled leaves (each set has two, three or five leaves). Like some in the Buttercup family, its flower lacks petals and instead has large petal-like sepals. In fall, its thimble-shaped seed head turns into a cottony tuft with many small seeds. American Indians used this plant medicinally for its expectorant properties.

FLOWER TYPE
Regular

LEAF TYPE
Simple Lobed

LEAF ATTACHMENT
Whorl

LEAF ATTACHMENT
Basal

239

Crowpoison

Nothoscordum bivalve

Family: Lily (Liliaceae)

Height: 4–12" (10–30 cm)

Flower: white to pinkish, 1" (2.5 cm) wide, of 6 similar-looking sepals and petals surrounding a green or yellow center; petals are oval, pointed at the tips and green at the base; groups of 5–12 flowers per plant

Leaf: narrow, 4–8" (10–20 cm) long, smooth margin, basally attached; hollow stem

Bloom: spring, summer

Cycle/Origin: perennial; native

Habitat: moist soils, open woods, old fields, roadsides, near granite and limestone rocks, sun

Range: throughout South Carolina, except in the western mountainous counties; eastern two-thirds of North Carolina

Notes: Genus name *Nothoscordum* means "false garlic," providing another common name and referring to the bulb from which it grows. This Lily family member has an onion-like appearance, but lacks any onion or garlic odor. The species name *bivalve* means "two-parted" and refers to the tiny fruit, which actually has three parts to its capsule. An abundant wildflower that blooms in spring, but often flowers again in the fall.

FLOWER TYPE **Regular** LEAF TYPE **Simple** LEAF ATTACHMENT **Basal**

Carolina Horsenettle
Solanum carolinense

Family: Nightshade (Solanaceae)

Height: 12–36" (30–91 cm)

Flower: white or lavender to purple, 1" (2.5 cm) wide, 5 pointed petals in star shape around protruding bright yellow flower parts; petals often white above, purple below with white stripe down the center; several flowers on each prickly flower stalk

Leaf: lance-shaped, lobed, 3–8" (7.5–20 cm) long, divided into 2–5 irregular pointed lobes (sometimes smooth edged), covered with star-shaped hairs, spines on veins above, spines on underside

Fruit: globular green- and yellow-streaked berry, turning yellow when ripe, ⅝" (1.5 cm) wide

Bloom: summer

Cycle/Origin: perennial; native

Habitat: dry sandy soils, disturbed areas, fields, lawns, sun

Range: throughout

Notes: Originally native to the Southeast, but found now throughout the U.S. It aggressively spreads by underground stems, forming large colonies. The fruit resembles a tiny tomato (also a member of the Nightshade family), but is poisonous and has killed deer, cattle and humans. Cherokee Indians used this plant medicinally, but also crushed its berries in sweetened milk to use as fly poison. Stems and leaves have large spines that can perforate skin, so handle with care.

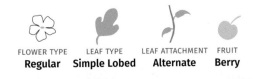

FLOWER TYPE
Regular

LEAF TYPE
Simple Lobed

LEAF ATTACHMENT
Alternate

FRUIT
Berry

fruit

Virginia Strawberry
Fragaria virginiana

Family: Rose (Roseaceae)

Height: 3–6" (7.5–15 cm)

Flower: white, 1" (2.5 cm) wide, 5 separated oval petals around a fuzzy yellow center; in sets of 2–10 flowers

Leaf: compound, 3–4" (7.5–10 cm) wide, whitish green, made up of 3 leaflets; each oval leaflet, 1–2" (2.5–5 cm) long, coarse-toothed margin; leaves sit on a tall hairy stalk

Fruit: green berry, turning bright red, ¼–½" (.6–1 cm) wide

Bloom: spring, summer

Cycle/Origin: perennial; native

Habitat: dry to moist loose soils, edges of woods, roadsides

Range: throughout North Carolina, western two-thirds of South Carolina

Notes: One of the two original species from which cultivated strawberries are derived and the only true wild strawberry in the Carolinas. Flowers are smaller than those of the garden variety of strawberry, which sometimes escapes into the wild. Often grows in large patches. Its flowers and fruit are always on stalks separate from the leaves. Produces some of the sweetest of the wild berries, which are high in vitamin C. The berries can be eaten fresh or made into jam.

FLOWER TYPE **Regular**   LEAF TYPE **Compound**   LEAF ATTACHMENT **Basal**   FRUIT **Berry**

Bouncing Bet
Saponaria officinalis

Family: Pink (Caryophyllaceae)

Height: 12–24" (30–61 cm)

Flower: white to pink, 1" (2.5 cm) wide, 5 ragged-tipped petals; in loose groups of 20–40 flowers; groups top 1 to several stems and grow from each upper leaf junction

Leaf: narrow, oblong to elliptical, 2–3" (5–7.5 cm) long and ½" (1 cm) wide, wavy margin, pointed tip, 3–5 conspicuous veins, attached directly to stem; oppositely attached, but can be in whorls of 3–4 leaves

Bloom: summer, fall

Cycle/Origin: perennial; non-native

Habitat: moist to dry soils, along railroads, ditches, stream sandbars, old fields, disturbed areas, sun

Range: throughout

Notes: Often seen growing in patches along roads. Its fragrant white (often pink) flowers look similar to those of phlox. Also called Soapwort because the roots contain saponin, a chemical that becomes slippery and sudsy when wet. Once used as a soap. Spreads by underground stems (rhizomes), but also produces large amounts of small purplish black seeds. Bouncing Bet makes a good garden plant, but be aware—it will spread.

CLUSTER TYPE **Round** FLOWER TYPE **Regular** LEAF TYPE **Simple** LEAF ATTACHMENT **Opposite** LEAF ATTACHMENT **Whorl**

Eastern Daisy Fleabane
Erigeron annuus

Family: Aster (Asteraceae)

Height: 1–5' (30–152 cm)

Flower: small white flower head, 1" (2.5 cm) wide, made of numerous (up to 100) tiny white-to-pink or lavender petals (ray flowers) surrounding a yellow center (disk flowers); each flower head sits atop flower stalk

Leaf: usually elliptical or narrowly lance-shaped, 1–5" (2.5–13 cm) long, smooth or coarse-toothed edges, hairy; attached directly to and alternately along the slightly to noticeably hairy multi-branched stem

Bloom: summer, fall

Cycle/Origin: annual; native

Habitat: moist or dry soils, roadsides, fields, along railroads, disturbed sites, sun

Range: throughout North Carolina, northeastern half of South Carolina

Notes: One of six fleabane species in the genus *Erigeron* found in the Carolinas, this plant is one of the most common and widespread. Eastern Daisy Fleabane is weedier and taller than Prairie Fleabane (*E. strigosus*) (not shown), which has smaller flower heads and narrower leaves. Fleabanes were so named because the dried foliage was said to kill fleas and bedbugs.

FLOWER TYPE LEAF TYPE LEAF ATTACHMENT
Composite **Simple** **Alternate**

Whitestar

Ipomoea lacunosa

Family: Morning Glory (Convolvulaceae)

Height: 3–9' (.9–2.7 m); vine

Flower: white to pinkish, 1" (2.5 cm) long, often with a purple center, trumpet-shaped, 5 fused petals widely flared outward with sharply pointed tips, purple flower parts (anthers)

Leaf: heart-shaped, 1½–3" (4–7.5 cm) long, sometimes 3 deeply cleft lobes, green with purple edges; alternately attached on a stalk; sparsely haired, twining, branching, reddish green vine

Fruit: spherical green capsule, turning brown, ½" (1 cm) wide, flattened on each end, stiff hairs

Bloom: summer, fall

Cycle/Origin: annual; native

Habitat: moist or sandy soils, disturbed sites, along roads and fences, thickets, stream banks, lakeshores, sun

Range: throughout

Notes: Although a fast-growing plant, the native Whitestar is not as invasive as some non-native species. However, its vines can still be a problem by choking the harvesting machines of cotton, corn, soybean or peanut farmers. The seeds are eaten by game birds such as Ring-necked Pheasant and Northern Bobwhite, but the leaves smell rank and are avoided by deer and rabbits. Sometimes called Small White Morning Glory.

FLOWER TYPE **Tube**   LEAF TYPE **Simple**   LEAF ATTACHMENT **Alternate**   FRUIT **Pod**

White Clover
Trifolium repens

Family: Pea or Bean (Fabaceae)

Height: 4–10" (10–25 cm)

Flower: round cluster, 1" (2.5 cm) wide, of 40–100 tiny pea-like white flowers tinged with pink; each flower, ¼" (.6 cm) wide; fragrant cluster found above leaves on a single long stalk

Leaf: compound, 1½" (4 cm) wide, composed of 3 round leaflets; each leaflet, ¼–½" (.6–1 cm) wide, characteristic crescent- or V-shaped dusty white marking, finely toothed, stalked; leaves alternately attached

Bloom: spring, summer, fall

Cycle/Origin: perennial; non-native

Habitat: cool moist clay or silt soils, fields, lawns, mountain meadows, pastures, roadsides, sun

Range: throughout

Notes: Well known for occasionally producing a four-leaf clover, White Clover is a Eurasian import that has found a home in lawns across North America. It spreads by an aboveground stem that roots at each leaf attachment (node). The genus name *Trifolium* describes its three leaflets, while the species name *repens* refers to its creeping growth habit. Look for the crescent- or V-shaped dusty white markings on its leaves to help identify this sometimes "lucky" plant. White Clover attracts bees and a number of butterfly species, including skippers, blues, sulphurs and hairstreaks.

CLUSTER TYPE
Round

FLOWER TYPE
Irregular

LEAF ATTACHMENT
Alternate

LEAF TYPE
Compound

253

Indianhemp

Apocynum cannabinum

Family: Dogbane (Apocynaceae)

Height: 12–36" (30–91 cm)

Flower: round cluster, 1" (2.5 cm) wide, of 2–10 tiny greenish white flowers; each flower, ⅓" (.8 cm) wide, made up of 5 triangular petals; cluster found at the end of erect stalk

Leaf: oval, 2–4½" (5–11 cm) long, yellow-green, toothless, often with a wavy margin

Fruit: thin pod-like green capsule, turning reddish brown, 3–8" (7.5–20 cm) long, opens along 1 side to release seeds attached to long tufts of white fuzz that carry seeds away on the wind

Bloom: summer

Cycle/Origin: perennial; native

Habitat: moist soils, along roads, deciduous woods, sun

Range: throughout

Notes: A tall perennial plant with a single main stem branching into many spreading stems. A close relative of milkweed, insects avoid this plant because of the thick milky poisonous sap in its stems and leaves. The sap contains cardiac glycosides, which cause fatigue, hot flashes and rapid heartbeat. American Indians used the fibrous bark (similar to hemp, the coarse fiber from cannabis plants) to make strong cords, hence its common name. Orioles also use the fibrous stems of old Indian Hemp to construct their basket-like nests.

CLUSTER TYPE	FLOWER TYPE	LEAF TYPE	LEAF ATTACHMENT	FRUIT
Round	**Regular**	**Simple**	**Opposite**	**Pod**

Painted Trillium
Trillium undulatum

Family: Lily (Liliaceae)

Height: 8–16" (20–40 cm)

Flower: white, 1–1½" (2.5–4 cm) long, 3 oblong pointed wavy-edged petals with a pink or red crescent near the base streaking toward outer tip; white center; 3 short pointed green sepals visible between petals; single erect flower atop flower stalk

Leaf: oval, 2–4" (5–10 cm) long, bluish green, sharply pointed tip; whorl of 3 leaves just below the flower

Fruit: oval green berry, turning bright red when ripe, ½–1" (1–2.5 cm) long

Bloom: spring

Cycle/Origin: perennial; native

Habitat: mountain forests (hemlock, pine or spruce), often near rhododendrons, shade to partial shade

Range: western mountainous counties of the Carolinas

Notes: The rarest trillium in South Carolina, but common in the North Carolina mountains. "Painted" in the common name refers to the uniquely bicolored petals, which makes it hard to confuse this flower with any other trillium bloom. Species name *undulatum* refers to the wavy petals. White Trillium (pg. 293) usually has all-white petals, but it can sometimes resemble Painted Trillium due to a virus-like organism that causes pink streaking in the petals. Most trillium seeds are dispersed and inadvertently planted by ants.

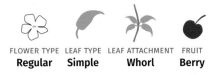

FLOWER TYPE	LEAF TYPE	LEAF ATTACHMENT	FRUIT
Regular	**Simple**	**Whorl**	**Berry**

Bloodroot

Sanguinaria canadensis

Family: Poppy (Papaveraceae)

Height: 5–10" (13–25 cm)

Flower: white (sometimes pink), 1½" (4 cm) wide, 8–10 petals and a golden yellow center; single large flower per plant atop a pinkish flower stalk

Leaf: round, 4–7" (10–18 cm) wide, with 5–9 lobes, bluish green, long stalk; usually solitary leaf wraps around flower stalk, opening out flat after blooming

Fruit: pod-like green capsule, 1" (2.5 cm) long, erect, smooth, beaked, contains 10–15 brown seeds

Bloom: early spring

Cycle/Origin: perennial; native

Habitat: rich deciduous woods, cliff bases, ravines

Range: throughout

Notes: One of the earliest sprouting plants, emerging from nearly frozen soil and flowering well before trees leaf out. Flower opens on sunny days, closing tightly at night. Its single leaf unrolls in full sun, curling up around the flower stalk at night and on cloudy days. These flowers lack nectar, quickly dropping petals after pollination and leaving a pointed pod-like capsule. The orangish red sap in the stems and roots was used by many cultures as a dye and an insect repellent. An extract from the sap in the roots is currently used in toothpaste for its plaque-fighting properties. Bloodroot is easy to grow in gardens from seed. Please do not dig it up from the wild.

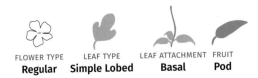

FLOWER TYPE
Regular

LEAF TYPE
Simple Lobed

LEAF ATTACHMENT
Basal

FRUIT
Pod

unripe fruit

ripe fruit

Mayapple
Podophyllum peltatum

Family: Barberry (Berberidaceae)

Height: 12–18" (30–45 cm)

Flower: white, 1–2" (2.5–5 cm) wide, 6–9 waxy petals; single nodding flower on a thin flower stalk rising from a crotch between the 2 leaves

Leaf: lobed, 12–15" (30–38 cm) wide, with 3–9 deep lobes, smooth or coarse-toothed margin; 2 oppositely attached leaves stand well above the flower

Fruit: lemon-shaped green berry, turning yellow when ripe, 2" (5 cm) wide

Bloom: spring

Cycle/Origin: perennial; native

Habitat: moist rich soils, thickets, shady meadows, moist woods, bottomlands, along railroads, partial shade

Range: throughout

Notes: A plant of rich woods and shady clearings, it grows in large colonies that can obscure the forest floor. Actually blooms in March and April in the Carolinas, with "May" in the common name referring to its blooming time farther north. The flowering of this plant has been used as an indicator of when to start looking for the elusive morel mushroom. Mayapple leaves, stems, roots and unripe fruit are toxic; however, the large lemon-shaped berries are said to be edible when ripe. The White Slant Line moth can often be seen resting in the blossoms for camouflage.

FLOWER TYPE
Regular

LEAF TYPE
Simple Lobed

LEAF ATTACHMENT
Opposite

FRUIT
Pod

FRUIT
Berry

Japanese Honeysuckle
Lonicera japonica

Family: Honeysuckle (Caprifoliaceae)

Height: 3–30' (.9–9.1 m); vine

Flower: pinkish white with pink base when first open, turning white, then yellow with age, 1–2" (2.5–5 cm) long, 2 petals (lips) fused to form a tube half the length of flower, spreading trumpet-like into fringed upper lip and undivided bottom lip; flowers in pairs

Leaf: oblong, 1½–3" (4–7.5 cm) long, evergreen, pointed tip, blunt base, hairy, edges sometimes toothed or lobed; on a clockwise-twining woody vine

Fruit: round green berry, black when ripe, ⅓" (.8 cm) wide, juicy, contains many seeds

Bloom: spring, summer

Cycle/Origin: perennial; non-native, from eastern Asia

Habitat: dry soils, thickets, abandoned fields, near old barns

Range: throughout

Notes: Introduced in the mid-1800s. Now naturalized throughout the eastern U.S., especially in disturbed sites. Fast growing and heavy, it can deform trees upon which it climbs. A spreading vine, it blocks sunlight from reaching other plants. Still planted by some, but considered invasive and banned from cultivation in four northeastern states. The natives Trumpet Honeysuckle (pg. 211) or Trumpet Creeper (pg. 215) are better alternatives for gardens—both have showy red flowers and are easily obtained.

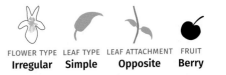

FLOWER TYPE
Irregular

LEAF TYPE
Simple

LEAF ATTACHMENT
Opposite

FRUIT
Berry

Corn Chamomile
Anthemis arvensis

Family: Aster (Asteraceae)

Height: 4–36" (10–91 cm)

Flower: white flower head, 1–2" (2.5–5 cm) wide, daisy-like, made up of 10–16 oblong petals (ray flowers) with 2 creases running lengthwise and 2–3 notches at each tip; flat orangish yellow center (disk flowers) becomes cone-shaped with age when the petals droop; 1 flower per stalk; many flowers per plant

Leaf: deeply lobed and fern-like, 1–2½" (2.5–6 cm) long, divided 2–3 times, pointed tips on lobes, fringe-like lobes at leafstalk base, alternately attached; many erect, multi-branched, hairy red or green stems

Bloom: summer

Cycle/Origin: annual; non-native

Habitat: sandy soils, waste ground, roadsides, old fields, sun

Range: throughout

Notes: Native to Europe, this shaggy, many-flowered weed has spread across the United States, especially in disturbed sites. The scentless flower head resembles a white daisy when it first blooms, but with age when the petals droop and the center becomes cone-shaped, it looks like a coneflower. A relative less common in the Carolinas, Stinking Chamomile *(A. cotula)* (not shown), has a strong odor, even more finely divided leaves and a center that becomes conical well before the petals wilt.

FLOWER TYPE
Composite

LEAF TYPE
Simple Lobed

LEAF ATTACHMENT
Alternate

Ox-eye Daisy
Leucanthemum vulgare

Family: Aster (Asteraceae)

Height: 12–36" (30–91 cm)

Flower: white-and-yellow flower head, 1–2" (2.5–5 cm) wide, made of 15–35 white petals (ray flowers) surrounding a yellow or orange center of disk flowers

Leaf: basal, lobed, dandelion-like, 1½–6" (4–15 cm) long, thick, dark green, clasps the stem; stem (cauline) leaf, 1–2" (2.5–5 cm) long, stalkless; stem leaves look like the basal leaves, but are smaller

Bloom: spring, summer

Cycle/Origin: perennial; non-native

Habitat: wet or dry soils, fields, along roads, pastures, waste areas, sun

Range: throughout

Notes: Also called Common Daisy, the Ox-eye Daisy is a cultivated European import that escapes often and is seen growing in patches along roads. Grows short and erect in poor soils; in rich soils, grows tall and falls over because of its weak stem, spreading out across the ground. Ox-eye Daisy contains pyrethrum, a chemical that repels insects and is used in organic pesticides. An interesting composite of many flowers appearing as one large flower. Each white petal is considered a separate flower, while the center yellow portion is composed of many individual disk flowers. Found throughout the Carolinas, but occurs less frequently in southern South Carolina.

FLOWER TYPE	LEAF TYPE	LEAF ATTACHMENT	LEAF ATTACHMENT	LEAF ATTACHMENT
Composite	**Simple Lobed**	**Alternate**	**Basal**	**Clasping**

Swamp Azalea
Rhododendron viscosum

Family: Heath (Ericaceae)

Height: 3–8' (.9–2.4 m); shrub

Flower: white to pale pink (sometimes light red), 1–2" (2.5–5 cm) long, 5 long triangular backward-curving petals fused into very long, red-haired sticky tube; sticky pink-and-white flower parts extend beyond the petals; in groups of 4–9 vase-shaped flowers

Leaf: oblong and lance-shaped or elliptical, 1–2½" (2.5–6 cm) long, bristly hairs, sharp pointed tip; deciduous; gray stem; more leaves toward the top of plant

Fruit: narrow, oval, light violet-to-reddish capsule, ½–¾" (1–2 cm) long, has many pale orange-yellow seeds

Bloom: summer

Cycle/Origin: perennial; native

Habitat: hummocks in swamps, pond margins, lakeshores

Range: throughout

Notes: Although called Swamp Azalea, this rhododendron prefers its roots to be slightly above the water line. Spread by runners, this multi-stemmed shrub is often found in wide colonies and grows 5 feet (1.5 m) tall. Its many sticky white flowers have a strong spicy fragrance that attracts moths and hummingbirds, which pollinate the blooms. Sometimes confused with Dwarf Azalea *(R. atlanticum)* (not shown), which flowers before and while growing leaves, is found mostly along the coast and is shorter than Swamp Azalea.

FLOWER TYPE **Tube**   LEAF TYPE **Simple**   LEAF ATTACHMENT **Alternate**   FRUIT **Pod**

White Snakeroot
Ageratina altissima

Family: Aster (Asteraceae)

Height: 1–5' (30–152 cm)

Flower: flat cluster, 1–2" (2.5–5 cm) wide, of 11–22 tiny fuzzy white flowers; each flower, ⅛" (.4 cm) wide; several clusters on branched stems

Leaf: broadly oval, 2–6" (5–15 cm) long, dark green, widest at leaf base, pointed tip, ragged teeth

Bloom: late summer, fall

Cycle/Origin: perennial; native

Habitat: moist soils, stream banks, shady disturbed sites

Range: western two-thirds of the Carolinas

Notes: Well known to be a late summer and a fall bloomer, White Snakeroot often grows along the shady edges of deciduous woods. Common in the mountains and hills of the Carolinas, but uncommon near the coast. Contains a toxic chemical that, if ingested by a cow, causes milk sickness. If humans then drink milk produced by that cow, they will also contract the disease, which is the very same sickness suggested to have killed Abraham Lincoln's mother. Today, because of better food availability for cows and modern processing, this is no longer a health concern. Many plants share "Snake" in their common names because of the belief that a plant growing in shade harbors snakes or because it may be used for snakebite treatment. Like other Aster family members, this plant has composite flowers made up entirely of disk flowers, lacking ray flowers.

CLUSTER TYPE	FLOWER TYPE	LEAF TYPE	LEAF ATTACHMENT
Flat	**Composite**	**Simple**	**Opposite**

Trailing Arbutus
Epigaea repens

Family: Heath (Ericaceae)

Height: 8–16" (20–40 cm)

Flower: tight round cluster, 1–2" (2.5–5 cm) wide, of many white-to-pink flowers; each flower, ¼–½" (.6–1 cm) wide, made up of 5 pointed flaring petals fused into short hairy tube; clusters near the ground

Leaf: oval, 1–3" (2.5–7.5 cm) long, evergreen, shiny dark green, thick, leathery; margins and stems covered with stiff rusty brown hairs

Fruit: globular fleshy brownish-red capsule, ½" (1 cm) wide, 5 segments split open to reveal tiny reddish orange seeds surrounded by a white pulp

Bloom: spring

Cycle/Origin: perennial; native

Habitat: rocky hillsides, oak woods, pinewoods, part shade

Range: throughout North Carolina, western two-thirds of South Carolina

Notes: A creeping plant with sweetly fragrant white (rarely pink) flowers. Begins to bloom in February in the Carolinas. Also called Mayflower, the Pilgrims who landed at Plymouth Rock greeted this plant as a harbinger of spring. Leaves (to a lesser extent, flowers) are often hidden beneath the fallen leaves of other plants. Ants eat the sweet pulp surrounding the seeds. Once common, but becoming rare because people pick the flowers and it is difficult to cultivate.

CLUSTER TYPE **Round** FLOWER TYPE **Regular** LEAF TYPE **Simple** LEAF ATTACHMENT **Alternate** FRUIT **Pod**

Heartleaf Foamflower

Tiarella cordifolia

Family: Saxifrage (Saxifragaceae)

Height: 6–12" (15–30 cm)

Flower: airy loose spike cluster, 1–2" (2.5–5 cm) long, of feathery white flowers; each flower, ¼" (.6 cm) wide, composed of 5 clawed petals

Leaf: somewhat maple-like, lobed, 2–4" (5–10 cm) long, divided into 3–5 shallow lobes with fine-toothed margins; basally attached on long leafstalk, 2–3" (5–7.5 cm) long; leaves and stems covered with fine white hairs; light green leaves turn bronze-colored in fall

Bloom: spring, summer

Cycle/Origin: perennial; native

Habitat: rich moist soils, deciduous woodlands, rocky outcroppings, shade

Range: western two-thirds of the Carolinas

Notes: Foamflower often forms colonies, spreading by underground stems (rhizomes). It is a good plant for shady yards and gardens because of its shade-loving nature. From a distance, its tiny feathery white flowers and white flower parts (stamens) resemble foam, giving rise to the common name. The genus name *Tiarella* is Greek and refers to the pistils, which look similar in shape to turbans worn by some ancient Persians.

CLUSTER TYPE	FLOWER TYPE	LEAF TYPE	LEAF ATTACHMENT
Spike	**Regular**	**Simple Lobed**	**Basal**

Redring Milkweed
Asclepias variegata

Family: Milkweed (Asclepiadaceae)

Height: 12–36" (30–91 cm)

Flower: slightly domed flat cluster, 1–2½" (2.5–6 cm) wide, of many small pure white flowers, each ⅓" (.8 cm) wide; 5 lower pinkish-tipped petals in a flat circle separated by a pink ring from 5 smaller upper petals raised above, resembling spokes of a wagon wheel

Leaf: broadly oval, 3–6" (7.5–15 cm) long, each end pointed, toothless, middle vein often tinged red

Fruit: elongated narrow green seedpod, turning brown, 4–5" (10–13 cm) long, releases many flattened seeds with silky white tufts that become airborne

Bloom: summer

Cycle/Origin: perennial; native

Habitat: dry soils, open woods, margins of upland woods

Range: throughout

Notes: The ring referred to in the common name is actually pink, not red. Over 100 milkweed species native to the U.S., all containing toxic cardiac glycosides in the milky sap. Sap is exuded when leaves, stems or flower stalks are broken. Monarch butterfly caterpillars feed only on milkweeds with no ill effects, but they and the resulting adult butterflies become bitter tasting and poisonous to birds and other animals. Despite the toxicity of the other plant parts, unopened pods that are nearly ripe have been cooked and eaten.

CLUSTER TYPE	FLOWER TYPE	LEAF TYPE	LEAF ATTACHMENT	FRUIT
Flat	**Irregular**	**Simple**	**Opposite**	**Pod**

Rabbit-tobacco

Pseudognaphalium obtusifolium

Family: Aster (Asteraceae)

Height: 12–36" (30–91 cm)

Flower: ragged flat cluster, 1–3" (2.5–7.5 cm) wide, of many conical white or yellowish flower heads, each ¼" (.6 cm) long; overlapping fuzzy white bracts with a few dark dull orange disk flowers in the center

Leaf: narrowly lance-shaped, 3" (7.5 cm) long, smooth margin, slightly hairy or sticky above, very hairy and whitish below, stalkless; many hairs closely pressed to greenish white stem; numerous leaves, progressively smaller near the top of stem

Bloom: summer, fall

Cycle/Origin: annual, biennial; native

Habitat: dry or sandy soils, open woods, clearings, forest edges, roadsides, along railroads, sun

Range: throughout

Notes: Rabbit-tobacco doesn't have showy flowers, but they are sweetly fragrant and last a long time when picked, thus it is aptly named. Leaves and flowers were once used to stuff pillows and mattresses and were also placed in linen cupboards, as the scent was thought to repel insects. According to nineteenth century medical texts, the entire plant had many medicinal uses. American Indians smoked the dried leaves as tobacco. Rabbits and White-tailed Deer eat the leaves.

CLUSTER TYPE
Flat

FLOWER TYPE
Composite

LEAF TYPE
Simple

LEAF ATTACHMENT
Alternate

Nodding Lady's Tresses

Spiranthes cernua

Family: Orchid (Orchidaceae)

Height: 4–20" (10–50 cm)

Flower: spike cluster, 1–7" (2.5–18 cm) long, of 20–40 densely packed, pearly white flowers; each slightly drooping flower, ½" (1 cm) long, partly obscured by pointed green bract; flowers in 3–4 columns twisting around the sticky hairy flower stalk

Leaf: basal, narrowly oblong, 4–8" (10–20 cm) long, 1–4 leaves at base; scale-like stem leaf, 1" (2.5 cm) long, pointed, smooth margin, alternate, closely clasping the stem; 3–8 leaves per stem

Bloom: summer, fall

Cycle/Origin: perennial; native

Habitat: open areas of bogs and swamps, wet disturbed areas

Range: scattered throughout the Carolinas

Notes: "Lady's Tresses" is for the shape of the flower spike, which resembles braided hair. *Spiranthes* is from the Greek *speira,* meaning "spiral." The basal leaves often wither before the plant flowers, but are sometimes present when in bloom. Readily forms large colonies, and hundreds to thousands of plants can be seen lining wet roadside ditches in late summer and in fall. Often found in disturbed areas. Also called Common Lady's Tresses or Autumn Lady's Tresses. The similar and often cultivated Marsh Lady's Tresses (*S. odorata*) (not shown) is taller, with flowers smelling of vanilla or jasmine.

CLUSTER TYPE	FLOWER TYPE	LEAF TYPE	LEAF ATTACHMENT	LEAF ATTACHMENT	LEAF ATTACHMENT
Spike	**Irregular**	**Simple**	**Alternate**	**Clasping**	**Basal**

flower

Downy Rattlesnake Plantain
Goodyera pubescens

Family: Orchid (Orchidaceae)

Height: 6–18" (15–45 cm)

Flower: dense cylindrical spike cluster, 1½–4" (4-10 cm) long, of 20–50 small white flowers surrounding the stalk; each flower, ¼" (.6 cm) long

Leaf: oval, 1–3½" (2.5–9 cm) long, evergreen, dark bluish green marked with network of conspicuous greenish white veins, wide white vein down the center, woolly; 4–8 leaves form a rosette at base

Fruit: oval green capsule, turning brown, 1" (2.5 cm) long, erect, hairy

Bloom: summer

Cycle/Origin: perennial, biennial; native

Habitat: acid soils, pine forests, upland oak woodlands

Range: throughout

Notes: One of the most common orchids in the Carolinas, but less common in the eastern half of each state. Slowly spreads by rhizomes, forming colonies when not disturbed. Evergreen leaves last for four years. Variegated leaves resemble markings on a rattlesnake's skin, thus "Rattlesnake" in its common name. The Latin *pubescens* means "downy," referring to the down on the flower and (possibly) the woolly leaves. Limited to the western mountains of the Carolinas, Lesser Rattlesnake Plantain (*G. repens*) (not shown) is very similar, but the flowers are along only one side of the flower stalk.

CLUSTER TYPE	FLOWER TYPE	LEAF TYPE	LEAF ATTACHMENT	FRUIT
Spike	**Irregular**	**Simple**	**Basal**	**Pod**

Hedge False Bindweed

Calystegia sepium

Family: Morning Glory (Convolvulaceae)

Height: 3–10' (.9–3 m); vine

Flower: white to pink, 2–3" (5–7.5 cm) long, 5 fused petals form the tubular or funnel-shaped flower

Leaf: arrowhead-shaped, 2–4" (5–10 cm) long, toothless; base of each leaf extends below its stalk attachment, giving the appearance of ears (basal lobes)

Fruit: nearly spherical, pod-like green container, turning tan and papery, ½" (1 cm) wide, contains 4 brown or black seeds

Bloom: summer

Cycle/Origin: perennial; native

Habitat: moist to wet soils, roadsides, marsh edges, along railroads, disturbed areas, woodlands, sun

Range: scattered throughout the Carolinas

Notes: A climbing vine that can grow as long as 10 feet (3 m), Hedge Bindweed is often seen on old fences and shrubs and in open fields. Classified as a noxious weed, this very aggressive vine pulls down and shades out other plants with stems that twist counterclockwise. Its flowers are highly variable in color, ranging from pure white to pink. The flowers open in the morning and close in the afternoon, usually lasting only one day. Hedge Bindweed is related to many other species of bindweed and morning glory in North America, including Tall Morning Glory (pg. 171).

FLOWER TYPE
Tube

LEAF TYPE
Simple

LEAF ATTACHMENT
Alternate

FRUIT
Pod

Man of the Earth

Ipomoea pandurata

Family: Morning Glory (Convolvulaceae)

Height: 3–15' (1–4.6 m); vine

Flower: white, 2–3" (5–7.5 cm) long and equally wide, trumpet-shaped, fused petals, burgundy center; 1–7 blooms per flower stalk

Leaf: heart-shaped, 2–6" (5–15 cm) long, stalked; alternately attached to a single vine or several twisting vines that are purplish and rise from the large root

Fruit: elliptical green capsule, turning brown, ½" (1 cm) long, stiff hairs

Bloom: summer

Cycle/Origin: perennial; native

Habitat: dry to moist soils, open woods, roadsides, along railroads, disturbed sites, thickets, lawns, fields, sun

Range: throughout

Notes: Also known by a more descriptive common name, Wild Potato Vine, for the slightly bitter tuber that resembles the cultivated sweet potato. The root is large, weighing up to 30 pounds (13.5 kg). A purgative when eaten fresh, but edible when roasted a long time. American Indians used the tuber as a staple in their diets and for medicinal purposes. Like most morning glory vines, it can be weedy and invasive and is a host plant for the Sweet Potato Weevil, a common garden pest.

FLOWER TYPE LEAF TYPE LEAF ATTACHMENT FRUIT
Tube   **Simple**   **Alternate**   **Pod**

Common Boneset
Eupatorium perfoliatum

Family: Aster (Asteraceae)

Height: 2–4' (61–122 cm)

Flower: flat cluster, 2–3" (5–7.5 cm) wide, of numerous tiny flat white flowers; each flower, ¼" (.6 cm) wide; white bristles give the cluster a fuzzy appearance

Leaf: large, lance-shaped, 4–8" (10–20 cm) long, pointed, toothed, hairy above and below; wrinkled opposing leaves join at leaf bases and enclose stem, appearing as if stem is growing through the leaves (perfoliate)

Bloom: spring, summer

Cycle/Origin: perennial; native

Habitat: moist to dry soils, ditches, along roads, meadows

Range: throughout

Notes: A tall plant common at roadsides, Boneset is easy to identify by its large crinkled paired leaves with large leaf bases that join around the stem, making the stem appear to be growing through one large leaf. Distinguished from the related Sweetscented Joe-pye Weed (pg. 129) and White Snakeroot (pg. 271) by its perfoliate leaves. To some healers, this odd leaf growth meant that the plant was useful for setting bones, hence its common name. The stem and leaves are covered with fine whitish hairs. Tea made from the leaves is said to relieve coughs and colds and break fevers. One of the plants blooming in late summer when many butterflies abound, providing nectar for Monarchs, crescents and fritillaries.

CLUSTER TYPE	FLOWER TYPE	LEAF TYPE	LEAF ATTACHMENT
Flat	**Composite**	**Simple**	**Perfoliate**

White Turtlehead

Chelone glabra

Family: Snapdragon (Scrophulariaceae)

Height: 12–36" (30–91 cm)

Flower: tight spike cluster, 2–3" (5–7.5 cm) long, composed of numerous white (sometimes lavender) flowers; each flower, 1–1½" (2.5–4 cm) long, 2 petals fused together form a tubular flower

Leaf: narrow, lance-shaped, ½–1" (1–2.5 cm) wide, sharp teeth, oppositely attached to stem

Bloom: summer, fall

Cycle/Origin: perennial; native

Habitat: wet soils, moist fields, wetlands, along streams, seeps, swampy woods, sun

Range: throughout

Notes: Found along streams and in wetlands, White Turtlehead often grows as a single stem topped with a cluster of large white flowers. The shape of the flower resembles the head of a turtle, hence the common name. The genus name *Chelone* is Greek for "tortoise." Look for the narrow sharp-toothed leaves that are oppositely attached to the stem to help identify this wildflower. A host plant for the very rare Baltimore Checkerspot butterfly. Due to loss of habitat, White Turtlehead is not as common as it once was, thus neither is the butterfly.

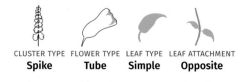

CLUSTER TYPE **Spike**   FLOWER TYPE **Tube**   LEAF TYPE **Simple**   LEAF ATTACHMENT **Opposite**

White Trillium
Trillium grandiflorum

Family: Lily (Liliaceae)

Height: 8–18" (20–45 cm)

Flower: white (turning pink), 2–4" (5–10 cm) wide, 3 wavy-edged triangular petals and 3 pointed green sepals (often mistaken for petals); single flower on 1 stalk

Leaf: large, broad, oval to diamond-shaped, 3–6" (7.5–15 cm) long, pointed tip, veins extend to edges of leaf; whorl of 3 leaves

Fruit: oval green berry, turning red when ripe, 1" (2.5 cm) long, grows singly

Bloom: early spring

Cycle/Origin: perennial; native

Habitat: rich moist soils, protected deciduous woods, shade

Range: westernmost mountainous counties of North and South Carolina (rare in South Carolina)

Notes: One of over 15 trillium species in the Carolinas. Has the largest flower of the trilliums, hence its common name. This is a protected species—please don't dig up the plant. Available for purchase, but get assurance the plants are cultivated from non-wild stock. Blooms early in spring, occurring alone or in groups. Its white flowers turn pink with age. White-tailed Deer eat the fruit, depositing seeds long distances away from the plant. Ants disperse seeds short distances by taking them to their under-ground homes to eat the oily outside coating only, allowing the seeds to germinate later.

FLOWER TYPE
Regular

LEAF TYPE
Simple

LEAF ATTACHMENT
Whorl

FRUIT
Berry

Common Yarrow
Achillea millefolium

Family: Aster (Asteraceae)

Height: 12–36" (30–91 cm)

Flower: tight flat cluster, 2–4" (5–10 cm) wide, of 5–20 white (sometimes pink) flower heads; each flower head, ¼" (.6 cm) wide, of 4–6 (usually 5) petals (ray flowers) surrounding a tiny center (disk flowers)

Leaf: fern-like, lobed, 4–6" (10–15 cm) long, finely divided, feathery; leaves have a strong aroma and become progressively smaller toward top of hairy stem; stalked lower and stalkless upper leaves

Bloom: summer, fall

Cycle/Origin: perennial; non-native

Habitat: dry soils, forests, open fields, disturbed sites, sun

Range: throughout

Notes: A common wildflower of open fields and along roads. A native of Eurasia as well as North America, it is uncertain whether these plants in the Carolinas were introduced or are native. Often confused with a type of fern because of its leaves. This plant grows in large clusters due to a horizontal underground stem. Genus name *Achillea* comes from the Greek legend that Achilles used the plant to treat bleeding wounds during the Trojan War. Species name *millefolium* means "thousand leaves," referring to the many divisions of the leaf, making one leaf look like many. Many cultures used it as a medicinal herb.

CLUSTER TYPE **Flat**   FLOWER TYPE **Composite**   LEAF TYPE **Simple Lobed**   LEAF ATTACHMENT **Alternate**

fruit

Devil's Darning Needles
Clematis virginiana

Family: Buttercup (Ranunculaceae)

Height: 6–10' (1.8–3 m); vine

Flower: delicate round cluster, 2–4" (5–10 cm) wide, of white flowers; each flower, 1" (2.5 cm) wide; 4–5 petal-like sepals around a center of many thin, greenish yellow, hair-like flower parts (stamens)

Leaf: compound, 6–8" (15–20 cm) long, made up of 3–5 oval or lance-shaped leaflets; each leaflet, 2" (5 cm) long, sharp-toothed margin or with lobes; leaves have purplish leafstalks

Bloom: summer, fall

Cycle/Origin: perennial; native

Habitat: moist soils, edges of deciduous woods

Range: throughout

Notes: One of nearly 20 species of *Clematis* found growing in eastern North America. A close relative of the garden clematis, this square-stemmed perennial vine is most commonly seen in the mountains and hills (rarely along the coast) of the Carolinas, often growing over fences or shrubs or along riverbanks. In late summer and in fall, the hairy plumes of its pollinated female flowers give the vine a frosted look. The seed head has curvy hair-like white projections, giving the plant the appearance of the beard of an elderly gentleman, hence another common name, Old Man's Beard. Please do not dig this plant up from the wild, as it can be grown from seed.

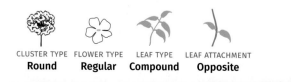

CLUSTER TYPE **Round**   FLOWER TYPE **Regular**   LEAF TYPE **Compound**   LEAF ATTACHMENT **Opposite**

Flypoison
Amianthium muscitoxicum

Family: Lily (Liliaceae)

Height: 12–36" (30–91 cm)

Flower: cone-shaped to cylindrical dense spike cluster, 2–5" (5–13 cm) long, of many white flowers; cluster elongating and turning cream, then green and finally purple or red with age; each flower, ½" (1 cm) wide, of 6 similar-looking petals and sepals

Leaf: many basal, long and thin, 16–24" (40–61 cm) long, blunt tip, smooth margin, arching downward; stem leaf, lance-shaped, much smaller or tiny (bract-like)

Fruit: fragile 3-chambered brown capsule, ¼" (.6 cm) long, contains shiny black or red seeds

Bloom: spring, summer

Cycle/Origin: perennial; native

Habitat: moist sandy soils, meadows, sandhills, bogs, oak woods, fertile forests, shade to partial sun

Range: throughout

Notes: After pollination, the flower spike of Flypoison persists and turns from white to cream to green, then finally to dark purple or red. All plant parts are toxic, especially the bulb. Early settlers crushed the bulb and mixed it with sugar to poison flies, thus its common name. Butterflies and other insect pollinators visit the flowers.

CLUSTER TYPE	FLOWER TYPE	LEAF TYPE	LEAF ATTACHMENT	LEAF ATTACHMENT	FRUIT
Spike	**Regular**	**Simple**	**Alternate**	**Basal**	**Pod**

flower

White Fringed Orchid
Platanthera blephariglottis

Family: Orchid (Orchidaceae)

Height: 12–36" (30–91 cm)

Flower: dome-shaped compact spike cluster, 2–6" (5–15 cm) long, of 20–30 pure white flowers; each flower, 1–1½" (2.5–4 cm) long, 1 upper sepal and 2 upper petals form a "hood," 2 sepals form side "wings," 1 lower tongue-like petal heavily fringed at tip and with a downward, backward-curving white spur

Leaf: elliptical and lance-shaped, 2–14" (5–36 cm) long, clasping the stem; 1–3 lower leaves; several upper leaves much smaller

Bloom: summer, fall

Cycle/Origin: perennial; native

Habitat: moist to wet soils, acid peat bogs, pine forests

Range: eastern third of the Carolinas

Notes: Orchids usually have flower parts united into a single column, but this orchid and others in the genus *Platanthera* (from the Greek words combined to mean "broad anthers") have two fang-like, yellowish, male flower parts that hang down from the "hood" of each flower (see inset). The slight spicy fragrance attracts moths, which drink the nectar and pollinate the flower. Growth requirements of most orchids are very specific and depend upon certain fungi being present in the soil, so don't dig up and transplant native orchid plants—they won't live long. Also called Porter Licorice Root.

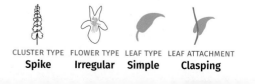

CLUSTER TYPE	FLOWER TYPE	LEAF TYPE	LEAF ATTACHMENT
Spike	**Irregular**	**Simple**	**Clasping**

leaf

Spotted Water Hemlock
Cicuta maculata

Family: Carrot (Apiaceae)

Height: 2–10' (.6–3 m)

Flower: umbrella-shaped flat cluster, 2–8" (5–20 cm) wide, made up of umbels of many tiny white flowers; each flower, ⅛" (.4 cm) wide; clusters at end of reddish branches; many clusters per plant

Leaf: compound, 3–10" (7.5–25 cm) long, divided 1–3 times into leaflets (upper leaves sometimes not divided); each lance-shaped leaflet, 1–4" (2.5–10 cm) long, toothed with leaf veins ending in the notch between the teeth, stalked; multi-branched stems are hollow, smooth and streaked with purple

Bloom: summer

Cycle/Origin: perennial, biennial; native

Habitat: wet soils, marshes, swamps, roadside ditches, pond edges, edges of lakes and creeks, sun to shade

Range: throughout

Notes: All parts of Spotted Water Hemlock are highly toxic to the nervous systems of humans and animals. It is considered the most poisonous plant native to North America, since consuming only a small amount can lead to death—even with immediate treatment. When cut, the stems and roots exude a yellow oil containing cicutoxin, a deadly substance that smells like carrots. Related to the plant that poisoned Greek philosopher Socrates.

CLUSTER TYPE **Flat**   FLOWER TYPE **Regular**   LEAF TYPE **Compound**   LEAF ATTACHMENT **Alternate**   LEAF ATTACHMENT **Clasping**

Atamasco Lily

Zephyranthes atamasca

Family: Lily (Liliaceae)

Height: 4–12" (10–30 cm)

Flower: white (becoming tinged with purple or pink), 3–4" (7.5–10 cm) long, trumpet-shaped, 6 similar-looking petals and sepals fused to form tube; petals flaring widely into equal-sized triangular lobes; central orange flower parts (anthers); grows singly on leafless stalk

Leaf: basal, flat and grass-like, 6–18" (15–45 cm) long, pointed tip, toothless, sharp edges; 4–6 drooping blades per plant

Bloom: spring

Cycle/Origin: perennial; native

Habitat: moist soils, rich woods, partial shade to full sun

Range: throughout South Carolina, eastern two-thirds of North Carolina

Notes: Most common along the Carolina coast and on the plateau between the coast and the mountains, Atamasco Lily announces spring with masses of white blooms along country byways and in moist pastures and bottomland forests. Early settlers called it Easter Lily for its habit of blooming in April, but it sometimes flowers even in midwinter. Veins of the white flower become tinged with pink after pollination. The leaves and bulb are poisonous. Also called Rain Lily for its habit of flowering after rain events.

FLOWER TYPE
Tube

LEAF TYPE
Simple

LEAF ATTACHMENT
Basal

Jimsonweed
Datura stramonium

Family: Nightshade (Solanaceae)

Height: 2–5' (61–152 cm)

Flower: white to lavender, 3–4" (7.5–10 cm) long, trumpet-shaped, 5 wavy-edged pointed-tipped petals fused to form tube; inside of tube heavily streaked with purple; green center; offensively acrid fragrance

Leaf: wedge- or arrow-shaped and lobed (can be irregularly toothed), 3–6" (7.5–15 cm) long, alternately attached to green, purple or red stem

Fruit: egg-shaped green capsule, turning brown, 2" (5 cm) long, erect, spiny to smooth, 4-parted, contains many black seeds

Bloom: summer, fall

Cycle/Origin: annual; non-native

Habitat: dry soils, disturbed areas, overgrazed fields, sun

Range: throughout

Notes: Also called Stinkweed for its noxious odor or Thornapple for the spiny fruit. All plant parts are poisonous and affect the nervous systems of mammals and humans when eaten, even killing livestock. Contains the alkaloids atropine and scopolamine, which can cause hallucinations, but are used medicinally. Some people develop a rash after touching the leaves. Said to be originally from Asia, but reported growing in Jamestown, Virginia, in the 1600s, fueling disagreement about its native or non-native status to the U.S.

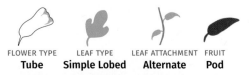

FLOWER TYPE
Tube

LEAF TYPE
Simple Lobed

LEAF ATTACHMENT
Alternate

FRUIT
Pod

fruit

Feathery False Lily of the Valley

Maianthemum racemosum

Family: Lily (Liliaceae)

Height: 12–36" (30–91 cm)

Flower: dense spike cluster, 3–5" (7.5–13 cm) long, of tiny star-shaped white flowers; each flower, ⅛" (.3 cm) wide, made up of 3 petals and 3 petal-like sepals, giving the appearance of 6 petals; cluster at the end of 1 long arching stem

Leaf: elliptical, 3–6" (7.5–15 cm) long, heavy parallel veining above, finely hairy below, pointed tip, smooth margin, mostly stalkless

Fruit: waxy green berry with red speckles, turning translucent red when ripe, ¼" (.6 cm) wide; clusters of several to many berries

Bloom: spring, summer

Cycle/Origin: perennial; native

Habitat: moist soils, deciduous woods, shade

Range: western three-quarters of the Carolinas

Notes: The spike flower cluster at the end of the stem distinguishes this plant from Smooth Solomon's Seal (pg. 49), which has flowers hanging from the stem at each leaf attachment. Grows on forest floors from an elongated horizontal underground stem. Its waxy red berries are not edible. A round scar on the stem (left after the stem has broken off) resembles the seal of King Solomon, hence the reference in the common name. Also called Solomon's Plume.

CLUSTER TYPE **Spike**   FLOWER TYPE **Regular**   LEAF TYPE **Simple**   LEAF ATTACHMENT **Alternate**   FRUIT **Berry**

flower

Queen Anne's Lace
Daucus carota

Family: Carrot (Apiaceae)

Height: 12–36" (30–91 cm)

Flower: flat cluster, 3–5" (7.5–13 cm) wide, of tiny white (sometimes pink or purple) flowers; each flower, ¼" (.6 cm) wide; usually a single purple-to-black floret near center of cluster; 3 thin forked green bracts below cluster

Leaf: twice compound, 8–10" (20–25 cm) long, of many leaflets on stalks; overall lacy fern-like appearance

Bloom: summer, fall

Cycle/Origin: biennial; non-native

Habitat: dry or disturbed soils, fields, along roads, sun

Range: throughout

Notes: Also called Wild Carrot and thought to be the ancestor of the common garden carrot. A European garden plant, it has escaped to the wild and is now considered a weed because of its aggressive growth. This tall plant has tiny hairs covering its stems. Beware: Queen Anne's Lace can be confused with the deadly Water Hemlock (pg. 303). Look closely for Queen Anne's central purple floret to help identify, but note that one variety does lack this feature. In its first year, the roots are soft enough to eat. Its long taproot has been roasted and ground to use as a coffee substitute. Host plant for Black Swallowtail butterfly caterpillars. Flower clusters dry and curl into a bird's nest shape and are often used in dried flower arrangements.

CLUSTER TYPE	FLOWER TYPE	LEAF TYPE	LEAF ATTACHMENT
Flat	Regular	Twice Compound	Alternate

fruit

Multiflora Rose
Rosa multiflora

Family: Rose (Rosaceae)

Height: 5–15' (1.5–4.6 m); shrub

Flower: slightly domed flat cluster, 3–8" (7.5–20 cm) wide, of many white-to-pinkish flowers; each flower, 1" (2.5 cm) wide, made of 5 heart-shaped petals around a yellowish center

Leaf: compound, made up of 7–9 elliptical leaflets; each leaflet, ½–2½" (1–6 cm) long, toothed margin; reddish fringe of many stipules at base of each leafstalk; curved flattened stiff thorns on arching stems

Fruit: globular green fruit, turning slightly yellow, then red when ripe, ¼" (.6 cm) wide, pulpy; hangs on the shrub until the next spring; referred to as a rose hip

Bloom: summer

Cycle/Origin: perennial; non-native, introduced from Asia

Habitat: dry soils, disturbed areas, woodland edges, sun

Range: throughout

Notes: Introduced as rootstock for cultivated roses, then used for living fences around barnyards or for erosion control. It escaped into the wild and invaded much of the eastern United States. Fringe at the base of each compound leaf distinguishes this rose from other rose species. Stems arch downward and root where the tips touch the ground, forming tangled thickets that block out native plants, but providing cover for wildlife. Petals and hips are edible.

CLUSTER TYPE
Flat

FLOWER TYPE
Regular

LEAF TYPE
Compound

LEAF ATTACHMENT
Alternate

FRUIT
Berry

fruit

Shepherd's Purse

Capsella bursa-pastoris

Family: Mustard (Brassicaceae)

Height: 4–24" (10–61 cm)

Flower: very loose spike cluster, 3–10" (7.5–25 cm) long, of white flowers; each small flower, ¼" (.6 cm) wide; flowers widely spaced along stem on horizontal stalks and densely packed at the top

Leaf: basal, oblong, 2–4" (5–10 cm) long, deeply lobed, fine-toothed margin; many basal leaves in rosette at base; a few much narrower stem leaves (cauline), lance-shaped, smooth edges or minutely toothed, clasping the single or branching stem; both types have star-shaped hairs at margins

Fruit: flattened heart-shaped or triangular green pod, turning tan to brown, ¼" (.6 cm) long

Bloom: spring, summer, fall

Cycle/Origin: annual; non-native, from Europe

Habitat: dry soils, disturbed areas, roadsides, pastures, sun

Range: throughout

Notes: Shepherd's Purse is commonly found in every state and considered an invasive weed. One of the earliest- and latest-flowering plants wherever it occurs. Its heart-shaped seedpods are typical of all plants in the Mustard family and are edible. The basal leaves that grow before the flower stalks appear can be eaten raw in salads or cooked as greens. Related to the common garden cabbage.

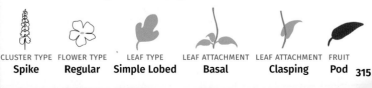

CLUSTER TYPE	FLOWER TYPE	LEAF TYPE	LEAF ATTACHMENT	LEAF ATTACHMENT	FRUIT
Spike	Regular	Simple Lobed	Basal	Clasping	Pod

Crimsoneyed Rosemallow

Hibiscus moscheutos

Family: Mallow (Malvaceae)

Height: 4–7' (1.2–2.1 m)

Flower: white or all pink, 4–7" (10–18 cm) wide, slightly cup-shaped, 5 wedge-shaped petals, magenta center outlined in pink, brilliant yellow flower parts; flower base held by pointed green sepals (calyx)

Leaf: egg- or lance-shaped, 6–8" (15–20 cm) long, grayish green and smooth above, white with soft hairs below, wavy; upper leaves irregularly toothed

Fruit: oval or rounded greenish capsule, turning reddish brown, 1½" (4 cm) long, tipped with short beak, partly enclosed by persistent brown calyx, contains dark brown seeds

Bloom: summer, fall

Cycle/Origin: annual, perennial; native

Habitat: wet to well-drained soils, swamps, roadsides, sun

Range: throughout

Notes: A many-flowered plant that grows in colonies of more than 200. Although a perennial in the wild, most of the fast-growing varieties have been cultivated as annuals and have flowers 9–12 inches (22.5–30 cm) wide, ranging from white to dark crimson. Each showy flower lasts only a day, but this is a colorful plant to use for mass plantings, as borders, or planting along streams or ponds. Less common in the mountainous western counties of the Carolinas.

FLOWER TYPE	LEAF TYPE	LEAF ATTACHMENT	FRUIT
Regular	**Simple**	**Alternate**	**Pod**

White Colicroot

Aletris farinosa

Family: Lily (Liliaceae)

Height: 24–36" (61–91 cm)

Flower: spike cluster, 4–8" (10–20 cm) long, of many vase-shaped, mealy white flowers; each tubular flower, ½" (1 cm) long, of 6 petals nearly totally fused together surrounding yellow-to-orange flower parts

Leaf: basal, lance-shaped, 3–8" (7.5–20 cm) long, light green, pointed tip, in a rosette or star shape

Fruit: oval green pod, turning brown, 1" (2.5 cm) long, contains numerous tiny black seeds

Bloom: late spring, summer

Cycle/Origin: perennial; native

Habitat: wet acid soils, upland woods, pinewoods, old fields

Range: throughout North Carolina, eastern half and western mountainous counties of South Carolina

Notes: Beloved by butterflies for its nectar, White Colicroot is a late spring flower commonly seen along highways and roads. Golden Colicroot (*A. aurea*) (not shown), which has yellow flowers, blooms several weeks later than White Colicroot in some of the same areas. Also called White Stargrass for the shape of the basal attachment of leaves, this is the colicroot most frequently found at the higher elevations of the Carolina mountains and sandhills. The plant was used by early American colonists to treat stomach ailments such as colic. Some folks still chew the root to alleviate a toothache.

CLUSTER TYPE	FLOWER TYPE	LEAF TYPE	LEAF ATTACHMENT	FRUIT
Spike	**Tube**	**Simple**	**Basal**	**Pod**

fruit

American Pokeweed

Phytolacca americana

Family: Pokeweed (Phytolaccaceae)

Height: 4–10' (1.2–3 m)

Flower: distinctive spike cluster, 6–10" (15–25 cm) long, with many white, greenish or pink flowers; each flower, ¼" (.6 cm) wide, has no petals, but has 5 petal-like sepals

Leaf: lance-shaped, 5–10" (13–25 cm) long, tapering at both ends, smooth margin, alternately attached

Fruit: whitish green berry, turning dark purple to black when ripe, ½" (1 cm) wide, flattened on each end; in drooping clusters on green (turning red) stem

Bloom: summer, fall

Cycle/Origin: perennial; native

Habitat: disturbed areas, clearings in damp woodlands, sun

Range: throughout

Notes: A large and obvious plant with a history of various uses. Emerging green shoots in spring were once gathered and cooked. However, as the plant matures, its leaves and shoots turn reddish and become toxic. Pokeweed berries (known as pokeberries) are named for the shape of the berry, which looks as if the ends were squeezed or "poked" together. The berries are poisonous to humans and livestock, but are consumed safely by birds. In the nineteenth century, pokeberry juice was used as a dye and as ink. Many letters were written with "poke" juice during the Civil War.

CLUSTER TYPE	FLOWER TYPE	LEAF TYPE	LEAF ATTACHMENT	FRUIT
Spike	**Regular**	**Simple**	**Alternate**	**Berry**

White Vervain
Verbena urticifolia

Family: Verbena (Verbenaceae)

Height: 1–5' (30–152 cm)

Flower: long thin spike cluster, 10–24" (25–61 cm) long, of white flowers; each tiny tube-like flower made up of 5 petals fused into a short tube, spreading into rounded lobes; flowers widely spaced and alternately attached along spike

Leaf: broadly lance-shaped, 2–6" (5–15 cm) long, wrinkled, coarse-toothed margin, sharply pointed tip, velvet-like short hairs, stalked; each pair of leaves rotated at right angles to next pair; 4-angled hollow hairy stem

Bloom: summer, fall

Cycle/Origin: annual, perennial; native

Habitat: dry sandy soils, old pastures, meadows, woods, roadsides, disturbed areas, partial sun

Range: throughout

Notes: The small white flowers of this very tall, skinny plant open a few at a time, so the spike is not showy, but it still attracts bees and small butterflies. Sparrows love the seeds. Species name *urticifolia* refers to the short nettle-like hairs on the stem and leaves. A tincture of the leaves was once used to treat bruises, poison oak and epilepsy. The similar-looking Narrowleaf Vervain (*V. simplex*) (not shown) has lavender flowers and narrower leaves than does White Vervain.

CLUSTER TYPE
Spike

FLOWER TYPE
Regular

LEAF TYPE
Simple

LEAF ATTACHMENT
Opposite

Flowering Spurge
Euphorbia corollata

Family: Spurge (Euphorbiaceae)

Height: 12–36" (30–91 cm)

Flower: flat cluster, 11–12" (28–30 cm) wide, of tiny white flowers; each flower composed of 5 bracts (often mistaken for petals) around a green-and-yellow center; each cluster sits atop a branch of the multi-branched flower stalk

Leaf: elliptical, 1–2½" (2.5–6 cm) long, smooth margin; stem leaves (cauline) mostly alternately attached, but upper leaves whorled around stem; slender stem containing milky sap

Fruit: oval white capsule, ⅛" (.4 cm) long, 3-parted and smooth

Bloom: spring, summer, fall

Cycle/Origin: perennial; native

Habitat: dry soils, fields, roadsides, woodland edges, sun

Range: throughout

Notes: Like all spurges, Flowering Spurge lacks both petals and sepals and actually has bracts that resemble petals. The poinsettia seen during Christmastime is a familiar example of a plant with petal-like red bracts that are often mistaken for petals. The milky sap in the stem is a purgative and was used by the Cherokee to treat many illnesses. It can also cause a rash in some people.

CLUSTER TYPE	FLOWER TYPE	LEAF TYPE	LEAF ATTACHMENT	LEAF ATTACHMENT	FRUIT
Flat	**Regular**	**Simple**	**Alternate**	**Whorl**	**Pod**

flower

Orangegrass
Hypericum gentianoides

Family: St. John's Wort (Clusiaceae)

Height: 4–20" (10–50 cm)

Flower: yellow, ½" (1 cm) wide, star-shaped, made up of 5 petals surrounding 5–10 protruding yellow flower parts (stamens); petals pale yellow at bases

Leaf: tiny, scale-like, pointed; opposite pairs pressed up against bluish green stem; numerous slim green branches rising from a central red stem; whole stem and leaves turning deep red in fall

Fruit: slender cone-shaped green pod, turning deep red, ⅛" (.4 cm) long, contains black seeds

Bloom: spring, summer

Cycle/Origin: annual; native

Habitat: sandy or rocky soils, near granite outcrops, sun

Range: throughout

Notes: "Orange" is for the citrus odor emitted when the stems are crushed. This erect herb is easily distinguished from the more than 30 other species in the St. John's Wort family in the Carolinas by its wiry bushy stems and small flowers. Also known as Pineweed for the leafless appearance of its stems in the summer. From above, the petals resemble propeller airplane blades. May be overlooked when blooming, as its flowers (although numerous) are small and close in the afternoon. More noticeable in fall when its tiny fruit become deep red, turning color before the stems and leaves.

FLOWER TYPE
Regular

LEAF TYPE
Simple

LEAF ATTACHMENT
Opposite

FRUIT
Pod

327

fruit

Seedbox
Ludwigia alternifolia

Family: Evening Primrose (Onagraceae)

Height: 1–4' (30–122 cm)

Flower: pale yellow, ½" (1 cm) wide, 4 nearly round petals surround an X-shaped center (stigma); 4 pointed purple-tinged green sepals (calyx) below and between petals; flower on a short stalk

Leaf: slim and lance-shaped, 2–5" (5–13 cm) long, gray-ish green below, turning red at tips in fall; widely spaced alternate leaves along multi-branched stem

Fruit: cube-like red container, ¼" (.6 cm) wide, round-bottomed, hairy or smooth; supported by persistent purplish green calyx, turning red in fall

Bloom: summer, fall

Cycle/Origin: perennial; native

Habitat: wet soils, swamps, ditches, seepages, disturbed sites

Range: throughout

Notes: Touch the flower or shake the flowering plant gently—if the petals drop off easily, you have found an Evening Primrose family member. Although there are 22 other species of Evening Primrose in the Carolinas, Seedbox is one of the most common and widespread. Almost showier in autumn than when blooming; the bracts turn reddish and remain on the plant after the petals drop, looking like pink blooms. Aptly named for its nearly cube-shaped fruit, which contains seeds that rattle when the ripe fruit is shaken.

FLOWER TYPE	LEAF TYPE	LEAF ATTACHMENT	FRUIT
Regular	**Simple**	**Alternate**	**Pod**

Java-Bean
Senna obtusifolia

Family: Pea or Bean (Fabaceae)

Height: 5–8' (1.5–2.4 m)

Flower: yellow, ½" (1 cm) wide, 5 unevenly sized oval petals; 1–2 drooping flowers grow from each upper leaf attachment (axis)

Leaf: compound, 6" (15 cm) wide, alternately attached, of 4–6 leaflets; each leaflet, 1½–2¾" (4–7 cm) long, flat and egg-shaped, oppositely attached, larger leaflets near end of stalk, smaller leaflets near base

Fruit: curved green pod, turning brown, 4–7" (10–18 cm) long, 4-angled, containing shiny dark brown seeds with diagonal stripes

Bloom: summer, fall

Cycle/Origin: annual, perennial; native

Habitat: woods, soybean fields, disturbed sites, sun

Range: throughout South Carolina, eastern half of North Carolina

Notes: The roasted seeds were once used as a coffee substitute, thus "Java" (an informal word for coffee) in the common name. Also called Coffee Bean. The leaves and seeds are toxic if eaten in large quantities by humans or livestock, and the entire plant smells rank. Species name means "blunt leaf," referring to the rounded ends of the leaflets. The edges of the leaflets curl inward at night or when cloudy. A troublesome weed, especially in agricultural fields.

FLOWER TYPE **Irregular**   LEAF TYPE **Compound**   LEAF ATTACHMENT **Alternate**   FRUIT **Pod**

Dwarf Cinquefoil
Potentilla canadensis

Family: Rose (Rosaceae)

Height: 2–6" (5–15 cm)

Flower: deep yellow, ½–¾" (1–2 cm) wide, made up of 5 bluntly fingernail-shaped, shallowly notched petals surrounding a yellow center; petals are separated (not overlapping), each on a short stalk; extremely hairy, pointed green bracts beneath the flower

Leaf: palmate, composed of 5 bluntly oval leaflets, 1½" (4 cm) long, sharply toothed margins on outer half of leaflets, appearing gray-green below due to numerous white hairs; long hairy reddish leafstalks

Bloom: spring, summer

Cycle/Origin: perennial; native

Habitat: dry acid or disturbed soils, edges of rocky upland woods, old fields, lawns, roadsides, sun

Range: throughout

Notes: Also called Five-fingered Grass, Dwarf Cinquefoil resembles a strawberry plant, but its leaves have five leaflets instead of three. The stem reaches a height of 6 inches (15 cm) in spring, but then topples over and creeps along the ground, growing as long as 20 feet (6.1 m). Sends out runners and roots at each node, often resulting in large masses covering the ground. Solitary flowers on erect flower stalks at leaf junctions. Hard to distinguish from the taller Common Cinquefoil (*P. simplex*) (not shown), which has longer leaflets.

FLOWER TYPE	LEAF TYPE	LEAF ATTACHMENT
Regular	**Palmate**	**Alternate**

Camphorweed

Heterotheca subaxillaris

Family: Aster (Asteraceae)

Height: 1–5' (30–152 cm)

Flower: yellow flower head, ½–1" (1–2.5 cm) wide, daisy-like, made up of 15–30 petals (ray flowers) and a yellow-orange center (disk flowers); many flower heads per plant atop the branched upper stem

Leaf: oval, 1–4" (2.5–10 cm) long, smooth or slightly toothed (can be wavy) margin, stalked and alternate lower on the stem, stalkless and clasping the middle and upper stem; leaves and the single stem are hairy and sticky due to glands in the hairs

Bloom: summer, fall

Cycle/Origin: annual, biennial; native

Habitat: dry sandy soils, dunes, open areas, disturbed sites, old fields, sun

Range: throughout the Carolinas, except in the western-most counties of North Carolina

Notes: This sparsely or densely leaved aster is named for the camphor-like odor emitted from its leaves when crushed. It is very weedy and drought tolerant. Farmers dislike it because cows avoid eating it, and the plant can take over pastures. However, it does serve as food for the caterpillars of several moth species. When applied to injuries, such as sprains or bruises, the foliage is said to diminish pain, inflammation and swelling.

FLOWER TYPE	LEAF TYPE	LEAF ATTACHMENT	LEAF ATTACHMENT
Composite	**Simple**	**Alternate**	**Clasping**

fruit

Indian Strawberry
Duchesnea indica

Family: Rose (Rosaceae)

Height: 3–12" (7.5–30 cm); vine

Flower: yellow, ½–1" (1–2.5 cm) wide, 5 widely spaced oval petals with notched tips, 5 pointed green sepals beneath and between the petals; flower sits above 5 green bracts that have 3 purple-tipped lobes; bracts turn slightly downward, white silky hairs below

Leaf: compound, 4½" (11 cm) long, made up of 3 oval leaflets; each leaflet, 2" (5 cm) long, round-toothed margin, long leafstalk; leaves alternately attached to trailing stem covered with white hairs

Fruit: strawberry-shaped green berry, turning red when ripe, ½" (1 cm) wide

Bloom: spring, summer, fall

Cycle/Origin: perennial; non-native

Habitat: moist soils, old fields, open woods, roadsides

Range: throughout

Notes: This low trailing vine was probably introduced from India, where it has been used to treat lung diseases and increase blood circulation. The outside of the fruit resembles a true strawberry, but the flesh inside is white, dry and tasteless. Not related to Virginia Wild Strawberry (pg. 245), which has sweet berries and white flowers. Unlike true strawberries, which are members of the genus *Fragaria*, Indian Strawberry is a member of the genus *Duchesnea*.

FLOWER TYPE	LEAF TYPE	LEAF ATTACHMENT	FRUIT
Regular	**Compound**	**Alternate**	**Berry**

Common Goldstar

Hypoxis hirsuta

Family: Lily (Lililiaceae)

Height: 4–24" (10–61 cm)

Flower: brilliant yellow, ½–1" (1–2.5 cm) wide, star-shaped, made up of 6 similar-looking petals and sepals, yellow above, greenish and hairy below; 2–6 flowers atop long leafless hairy stalk, 16" (40 cm) long

Leaf: long and thin, grass-like, 4–24" (10–61 cm) long, hairy, basally attached; leaves are longer than the flower stalks

Bloom: spring, summer

Cycle/Origin: perennial; native

Habitat: dry or moist soils, open woods, meadows, fields, old ruts made by wagons, sun

Range: throughout

Notes: This pretty little plant is often called Yellow Stargrass for the star-shaped flowers and grassy leaves. Its flowers, located well below the leaves, open early in the morning and often wilt by the afternoon. There are several other stargrasses widespread in the Carolinas that are hard to distinguish from each other and may be variations of the same species. Look for the hairy leaves to help identify. A good choice for the front border of a flower garden since it blooms throughout the summer. Self-seeds, but it takes the plants 1–3 seasons of growth to bloom.

FLOWER TYPE
Regular

LEAF TYPE
Simple

LEAF ATTACHMENT
Basal

Cutleaf Coneflower

Rudbeckia laciniata

Family: Aster (Asteraceae)

Height: 5–8' (1.5–2.4 m)

Flower: yellow flower head, ¾–1" (2–2.5 cm) wide, composed of a cone-shaped green center (disk flowers) encircled by 8–12 floppy petals (ray flowers); each flower head on tall flower stalk; each plant grows 20–50 large flower heads

Leaf: lobed lower, 5–16" (13–40 cm) long, divided into 3–7 sharp lobes, coarse teeth; simple upper, 2–3" (5–7.5 cm) long, coarsely toothed, nearly clasping the stem

Bloom: summer, fall

Cycle/Origin: perennial; native

Habitat: rich moist soils, fields, meadows, deciduous forests, edges of bogs, stream banks, partial shade

Range: throughout

Notes: A tall and robust perennial, Cutleaf Coneflower grows in moist soils. Look for its green center (cone) and drooping yellow petals, along with the lobed lower leaves and simple upper leaves, to help identify. Often seen growing in ditches, along roads or near old homesteads. A good plant for a butterfly garden. Its flowers attract butterflies such as Monarchs, which drink the nectar. Also known as Green-headed Coneflower or Golden Glow.

FLOWER TYPE
Composite

LEAF TYPE
Simple

LEAF TYPE
Simple Lobed

LEAF ATTACHMENT
Alternate

341

Queendevil Hawkweed

Hieracium gronovii

Family: Aster (Asteraceae)

Height: 1–5' (30–152 cm)

Flower: yellow flower head, ¾" (2 cm) wide, dandelion-like, made up of 20–40 petals (ray flowers), lacking disk flowers; each square-tipped petal has 5 lobes; green or purplish bracts, ½" (1 cm) long, tightly enclose the bases of the petals

Leaf: basal, broadly lance-shaped or teardrop-shaped, 1½–8" (4–20 cm) long, forming a rosette; a few shorter stem leaves, stalkless, alternately attached to lower stem; both types hairy with reddish bases; leafless green upper stem, lower stem dark purplish and hairy

Bloom: summer, fall

Cycle/Origin: perennial; native

Habitat: dry sandy or rocky soils, open woods, fields

Range: throughout

Notes: It is difficult to distinguish among hawkweed species with a casual glance as the flower heads appear similar, so look closely at the leaves of Queendevil Hawkweed to help identify. This plant is a food source for a variety of wildlife. Wild Turkeys eat the ripe seed heads, the foliage is consumed by deer and rabbits and the yellow flower heads attract bees.

FLOWER TYPE **Composite** LEAF TYPE **Simple** LEAF ATTACHMENT **Alternate** LEAF ATTACHMENT **Basal**

Sulphur Cinquefoil

Potentilla recta

Family: Rose (Rosaceae)

Height: 12–36" (30–91 cm)

Flower: pale yellow, yellow or white, 1" (2.5 cm) wide, 5 deeply notched heart-shaped petals surrounding dark orange or yellow flower parts, hairy pointed green bracts beneath flower; many flowers grouped loosely atop tall branching stem

Leaf: palmate; lower leaves made up of 5–7 leaflets; each oblong leaflet, 2–4" (5–10 cm) long, hairy below, sharply and deeply toothed to the base, stalked; upper leaves made up of 3 stalkless shorter leaflets; long white hairs on stout erect branched stem

Bloom: summer

Cycle/Origin: perennial; non-native

Habitat: dry soils, old fields, meadows, disturbed sites

Range: throughout

Notes: This showy flower was introduced from Europe and has escaped to colonize waste ground throughout most of the United States. Please do not plant this species—due to its ability to send out runners as long as 20 feet (6.1 m), it can form quite large clumps that compete with native grasses and overtake an area. Not well liked by farmers because livestock do not eat this plant. The native Dwarf Cinquefoil (pg. 333) is shorter than Sulphur Cinquefoil, and its petals have a much shallower notch.

FLOWER TYPE **Regular**   LEAF TYPE **Palmate**   LEAF ATTACHMENT **Alternate**

Bristly Buttercup

Ranunculus hispidus

Family: Buttercup (Ranunculaceae)

Height: 12–36" (30–91 cm)

Flower: bright yellow, 1" (2.5 cm) wide, 5 round petals; showy flowers grow on erect stalks above the leaves

Leaf: lobed, 3–4" (7.5–10 cm) wide, 3 distinct lobes are further divided into 3 lobes with sharp teeth; leaves on long hairy stalks, basally and alternately attached to hairy stem

Fruit: beaked green pod, ¼–½" (.6–1 cm) long, contains a winged seed; pods in cylindrical clusters

Bloom: spring, summer

Cycle/Origin: perennial; native

Habitat: rich soils, upland deciduous woods, springs, boggy areas, wet meadows, swamps, sun to partial shade

Range: western two-thirds of the Carolinas, scattered locations near the coast

Notes: A large robust plant with long hollow arching stems. Often spreads by rooting where its stems touch the ground, eventually forming large clusters. Bristly Buttercup is very deeply rooted and difficult to remove if grown in a garden. The common name comes from the long white hairs on its stems, leaves and the cup-shaped "buttery" yellow flowers. Also called Swamp Buttercup for its habit of growing in wet soils. Flowers produce little nectar, but much pollen, thereby attracting pollen-eating beetles, flies and bees.

FLOWER TYPE
Regular

LEAF TYPE
Simple Lobed

LEAF ATTACHMENT
Alternate

LEAF ATTACHMENT
Basal

FRUIT
Pod

flower

Wild Radish

Raphanus raphanistrum

Family: Mustard (Brassicaceae)

Height: 12–36" (30–91 cm)

Flower: yellow or white (can be violet, pink or orange), 1" (2.5 cm) wide, cross-shaped, made up of 4 oblong purple-veined petals around yellow center

Leaf: basal, oblong, 6–8" (15–20 cm) long, wider and toothed toward tip, deep irregular lobes at base; stem leaf smaller, slightly toothed or smooth-edged; both types stalked; erect bristly haired stem

Fruit: long narrow green pod, turning brown, 1–2½" (2.5–6 cm) long, beaked, flattened between seeds, ridged lengthwise

Bloom: spring, summer

Cycle/Origin: annual, biennial; non-native

Habitat: moist to dry soils, disturbed sites, roadsides, sun

Range: throughout

Notes: This introduced invasive conspicuous flower often blooms in masses along country roadsides in spring. Less commonly found in the mountainous western counties of the Carolinas. Genus name is from the Greek words for "quickly appearing," referring to the rapid germination of the seeds. Closely related to and may even be the ancestor of the garden radish, which has pink flowers. Lacks the familiar globular taproot of the garden radish, but all young plant parts are edible. Resembles wild mustards in the genus *Brassica*.

FLOWER TYPE	LEAF TYPE	LEAF TYPE	LEAF ATTACHMENT	LEAF ATTACHMENT	FRUIT
Regular	**Simple**	**Simple Lobed**	**Alternate**	**Basal**	**Pod**

349

St. Andrew's Cross

Hypericum hypericoides

Family: St. John's Wort (Clusiaceae)

Height: 2–4' (61–122 cm); shrub

Flower: pale yellow, 1" (2.5 cm) wide, 4 slim petals in shape of a cross backed by 2 unequal-sized pair of green sepals (calyx); many long thin protruding flower parts; each flower grows singly just above top leaves

Leaf: narrowly oblong, ¼–1" (.6–2.5 cm) long, firm (nearly succulent), many translucent dots above, smooth margin, narrow base; leaf length varies

Fruit: elliptical red pod, ⅙–⅜" (.4–.9 cm) long, containing black seeds; nearly enclosed by persistent red calyx that turns brown in winter

Bloom: summer, fall

Cycle/Origin: perennial; native

Habitat: dry to moist sandy or rocky soils, pinewoods, bogs

Range: throughout

Notes: Common name is for the arrangement of the petals, which resembles the cross of St. Andrew, the patron saint of Scotland. Over 30 species in the St. John's Wort family in the Carolinas, most of which have yellow flowers with 4–5 petals, many protruding stamens and leaves dotted with tiny oil-filled glands, thus making it hard to distinguish each. American Indians used the leaves, roots and bark to make medicines for pain, fever, dysentery or snakebite.

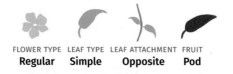

FLOWER TYPE	LEAF TYPE	LEAF ATTACHMENT	FRUIT
Regular	**Simple**	**Opposite**	**Pod**

Slender Scratch Daisy

Croptilon divaricatum

Family: Aster (Asteraceae)

Height: 8–36" (20–91 cm)

Flower: yellow flower head, 1" (2.5 cm) wide, daisy-like, made up of 7–11 (usually 8) petals (ray flowers) surrounding a yellow center (disk flowers); many flower heads per plant

Leaf: lance-shaped, 1–3" (2.5–7.5 cm) long, broader toward the tip, spiny-toothed margin; smaller leaves toward top of stem; leaves alternately attached to very branched, hairy green stalk; some stem hairs are hard and sharp

Bloom: summer, fall

Cycle/Origin: annual; native

Habitat: dry or clay soils, sandy loam, sandhills, pine-oak or hickory woods, roadsides, fencerows, sun

Range: throughout South Carolina, eastern half of North Carolina

Notes: The slender branches of this plant and the scratchy nature of its stem hairs explain its common name and makes Slender Scratch Daisy easily identifiable. Its flowers are diffuse on the plant and sit on very thin branches, appearing almost as if they are floating in midair. Sometimes a spreading invasive weed, it can form large colonies in disturbed areas. In the fall, it can be the most numerous of plants blooming on the plains near the Carolina coast.

FLOWER TYPE **Composite** LEAF TYPE **Simple** LEAF ATTACHMENT **Alternate**

Sneezeweed
Helenium amarum

Family: Aster (Asteraceae)

Height: 8–36" (20–91 cm)

Flower: yellow flower head, 1" (2.5 cm) wide, daisy-like, 5–10 fan-shaped drooping petals (ray flowers) circling a mounded yellow or brown center (disk flowers); each petal tip is 3-lobed; 8 narrow pointed green bracts dangle below flower head

Leaf: long and very narrow, 1–3" (2.5–7.5 cm) long and ⅛" (.4 cm) wide, smooth margin; numerous leaves; sometimes smaller clusters of leaves near each junction (axis) of the larger leaves; hairy red stems

Bloom: summer, fall

Cycle/Origin: annual; native

Habitat: dry sandy or poor soils, disturbed sites, meadows, old fields, roadsides, along railroads, sun

Range: throughout, except in the westernmost counties of North Carolina

Notes: An aromatic wide-ranging weed, Sneezeweed has spread across the eastern United States and the Midwest. Often found in disturbed or waste areas such as abandoned yards or gravel pits. It contains toxins that make it unpalatable to humans and livestock; cows will graze upon the plant in poor pasture, but then will produce tainted, bitter milk. A robust plant with long-blooming flowers, it is a good choice for cultivation in wildflower meadows.

FLOWER TYPE   LEAF TYPE   LEAF ATTACHMENT
Composite   **Simple**   **Alternate**

Spiny Sowthistle
Sonchus asper

Family: Aster (Asteraceae)

Height: 1–6' (.3–1.8 m)

Flower: yellow flower head, 1" (2.5 cm) wide, dandelion-like, made up of slender petals (ray flowers) with fringed tips; many flower heads per plant

Leaf: lance- or spoon-shaped, 2½–6" (6–15 cm) long, shiny dark green, stiff, very wavy and spiny margin, sometimes lobed (often deeply), curled rounded base clasping the stem; upper leaves much smaller, unlobed or shallowly lobed; round, branching, ridged, purplish green stem has milky sap

Bloom: spring, summer, fall

Cycle/Origin: annual; non-native

Habitat: dry soils, disturbed sites, along railroads, roadsides, fencerows, old fields, sun

Range: throughout

Notes: An introduced plant that has become a very invasive weed, spreading over much of the United States. Like a dandelion, its seeds are dispersed by the wind. Due to its deep taproot and spiny leaves, this stout plant is hard to eradicate. Cows avoid the annual because it is so spiny, allowing it to overrun fields. A look-alike, Common Sowthistle *(S. oleraceus)* (not shown), is less spiny than Spiny Sowthistle and has a curled leaf base that tapers to a point at the outside of the curl, unlike the ear-shaped leaf base of this plant.

FLOWER TYPE	LEAF TYPE	LEAF TYPE	LEAF ATTACHMENT	LEAF ATTACHMENT
Composite	**Simple**	**Simple Lobed**	**Alternate**	**Clasping**

Perfoliate Bellwort
Uvularia perfoliata

Family: Lily (Liliaceae)

Height: 8–16" (20–40 cm)

Flower: pale yellow, 1" (2.5 cm) long, bell-shaped, 3 pointed narrow petals overlapped by 3 similar petal-like sepals; orange granules on the inside surface; each flower grows singly; 1–3 flowers per plant

Leaf: elliptical, 2–3½" (5–9 cm) long, pointed tip, bright green, smooth below, stem appears to pass directly through the leaf base (perfoliate)

Bloom: spring

Cycle/Origin: perennial; native

Habitat: moist soils, deciduous woods, lowlands, shade

Range: western two-thirds of the Carolinas

Notes: The species name *perfoliata* and "Perfoliate" in the common name refer to the way in which the stem appears to perforate each leaf at its base. Bellworts spread by underground stems and are found growing in colonies. One of five species of bellwort found in the Carolinas (four of which are common), but only Perfoliate Bellwort has orange bumps on the petals and perfoliate leaves. Bellworts were once used to treat sore throats, and the young asparagus-like shoots were eaten after removing the leaves.

FLOWER TYPE
Bell

LEAF TYPE
Simple

LEAF ATTACHMENT
Alternate

LEAF ATTACHMENT
Perfoliate

Dogtooth Violet

Erythronium americanum

Family: Lily (Liliaceae)

Height: 5–10" (13–25 cm)

Flower: yellow and maroon, 1" (2.5 cm) wide, composed of 6 backward-curving petals (actually 3 petals and 3 sepals) surrounding conspicuous dangling maroon, brown or yellow flower parts (anthers)

Leaf: elliptical, 4–8" (10–20 cm) long, mottled with brownish purple spots and streaks, fleshy, pointed tip, 1–2 leaves per plant

Fruit: egg-shaped pod-like green capsule, turning brown, ½" (1 cm) long, flattened, 3-parted

Bloom: spring

Cycle/Origin: perennial; native

Habitat: rich moist soils, deciduous woods, part to full shade

Range: western two-thirds of the Carolinas

Notes: Also called Yellow Trout Lily for its tooth-shaped bulb, but Dogtooth Violet is a Lily family member and is not a violet. "Trout" comes from its mottled leaves, which resemble the spotting on the sides of a Brown Trout. Often found carpeting deciduous forest floors, it reproduces mostly by underground bulbs and forms extensive slow-growing colonies. May take up to seven years to mature enough to flower.

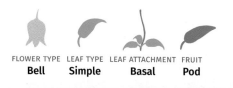

FLOWER TYPE	LEAF TYPE	LEAF ATTACHMENT	FRUIT
Bell	**Simple**	**Basal**	**Pod**

Partridge Pea
Chamaecrista fasciculata

Family: Pea or Bean (Fabaceae)

Height: 12–24" (30–61 cm)

Flower: yellow, 1–1½" (2.5–4 cm) wide, 5 teardrop-shaped petals, 5 pointed green sepals and a dark red center (stamens); 4 upper petals have a dark red base (1 of the outer petals curves back over center), up to 6 flowers in a row along the main stem at each leaf attachment (axis)

Leaf: compound, 2–3" (5–7.5 cm) long, delicate, feather-like, made up of 10–15 pair of oval leaflets; each leaflet, ½" (1 cm) long; leaves alternately attached along the erect reddish main stem

Fruit: pod-like green container, turning brown, 1–2½" (2.5–6 cm) long, thin, flat, hairy, contains 12 seeds; looks similar to that of the common garden pea

Bloom: summer, fall

Cycle/Origin: annual; native

Habitat: dry soils, disturbed areas, open thickets, meadows

Range: throughout

Notes: This Pea family member doesn't have the characteristic pea flowers—its almost equal-sized petals lay flat. The leaves fold up in direct sun, hence it is also called Sensitive Pea. Common, it grows in a wide variety of habitats throughout the Carolinas. A host plant for Little Yellow, Cloudless Sulphur, Gray Hairstreak and Ceraunus Blue butterflies.

FLOWER TYPE **Irregular**   LEAF TYPE **Compound**   LEAF ATTACHMENT **Alternate**   FRUIT **Pod**

Hairy Cat's Ear
Hypochaeris radicata

Family: Aster (Asteraceae)

Height: 6–24" (15–61 cm)

Flower: yellow flower head, 1–1½" (2.5–4 cm) wide, dandelion-like, of 20–30 slim yellow petals (ray flowers); outer spreading petals are washed with maroon below and have 5-lobed tips; erect and feathery inner petals; layers of pointed slim bracts with coarse hairs on middle veins tightly cup flower head

Leaf: spoon-shaped, deeply lobed (may be unlobed), 2–5½" (5–14 cm) long, wavy or toothed margin; coarse white hairs above and below; branching stems

Bloom: spring, summer

Cycle/Origin: perennial; non-native, from Europe

Habitat: dry sandy soils, disturbed sites, sun

Range: throughout North Carolina, northern counties of South Carolina

Notes: Often called False Dandelion as its flower head is so similar to Common Dandelion (pg. 377), but the true dandelion has smooth leaves and non-branching stems. Grows in large bunches and is extremely aggressive; it is listed as an invasive weed by several states. Stem and leaves contain a milky sap that reportedly is poisonous to horses, but pigs seek out and eat the fleshy roots with no apparent harm.

FLOWER TYPE
Composite

LEAF TYPE
Simple Lobed

LEAF ATTACHMENT
Basal

365

Green and Gold

Chrysogonum virginianum

Family: Aster (Asteraceae)

Height: 6–20" (15–50 cm)

Flower: golden yellow flower head, 1–1½" (2.5–4 cm) wide, daisy-like, made up of 5 slightly notched petals (ray flowers) surrounding a golden yellow center (disk flowers); flower head on long stem attached at leaf axis

Leaf: oval, 1–4" (2.5–10 cm) long, semi-evergreen, deep green, hairy, blunt-toothed margin

Bloom: spring, summer, fall

Cycle/Origin: perennial; native

Habitat: moist to somewhat dry soils, rich forests, sun to partial shade

Range: throughout

Notes: Green and Gold lives in rich moist woods in the wild. A native to the eastern United States, this low-growing perennial plant is often cultivated as ground cover and is especially valued for its many long-lasting blossoms. However, the plant is not drought tolerant—a drawback to cultivation. There are two varieties: one that spreads (best for ground cover) and a type that is more erect.

FLOWER TYPE **Composite** LEAF TYPE **Simple** LEAF ATTACHMENT **Opposite**

Common Sneezeweed

Helenium autumnale

Family: Aster (Asteraceae)

Height: 3–5' (.9–1.5 m)

Flower: bright yellow flower head, 1–2" (2.5–5 cm) wide, of 10–15 fan-shaped petals (ray flowers) and a yellow-green center (disk flowers); each petal tip has 3 lobes; the conspicuous ball-like center protrudes above the petals; up to 100 flower heads per plant

Leaf: narrowly lance-shaped, 3–6" (7.5–15 cm) long and ½–1" (1–2.5 cm) wide, stalkless, with widely and irregularly spaced teeth; edge of leaf base forms wings extending down the main stem

Bloom: fall

Cycle/Origin: perennial; native

Habitat: wet or clay soils, swamps, wet meadows, sun

Range: throughout

Notes: This plant often grows in a large dense clump and produces many flowers. Its ball-like center of disk flowers and unusually long leaf base edges (wings) help identify this member of the Aster family. Reportedly makes farm animals ill if eaten. Its dried leaves were once used as snuff and induced sneezing, thus "Sneeze" in the common name. Similar to Purplehead Sneezeweed (pg. 379), which is also found in wet soils in the Carolinas, but Purplehead Sneezeweed has a brownish purple flower center. Species name *autumnale* refers to the time of year when this plant blooms.

FLOWER TYPE
Composite

LEAF TYPE
Simple

LEAF ATTACHMENT
Alternate

Evening Trumpetflower

Gelsemium sempervirens

Family: Logania (Loganiaceae)

Height: 3–20' (.9–6.1 m); vine

Flower: brilliant yellow, 1–2" (2.5–5 cm) long, trumpet-shaped, 5 petals fused at bases and halfway along the length to form tube, short stalk; some flowers point upward, some droop

Leaf: oval, 1–3" (2.5–7.5 cm) long, smooth, shiny; semi-evergreen, turning bronze-colored in autumn; wiry red stem

Fruit: flattened elliptical green seedpod, turning reddish brown, 1" (2.5 cm) long, grooved down the middle

Bloom: early spring, summer

Cycle/Origin: perennial; native

Habitat: dry to wet soils, thickets, gardens, swamps

Range: throughout

Notes: South Carolina's official state flower, this twisting woody vine climbs trees or trails along fencerows, displaying bright fragrant flowers in early spring. American Indians used the root in a salve and as a blood purifier, but all of the plant parts are highly toxic. Sap contains alkaloids related to strychnine that can cause skin rashes on contact. Honey made from the nectar can kill if consumed. Nonetheless, Eastern Tiger Swallowtail butterflies and many bee species drink the nectar without any apparent ill effects. Also called Carolina Jessamine.

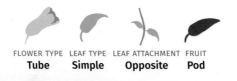

FLOWER TYPE
Tube

LEAF TYPE
Simple

LEAF ATTACHMENT
Opposite

FRUIT
Pod

color variation

Canadian Lousewort

Pedicularis canadensis

Family: Snapdragon (Scrophulariaceae)

Height: 5–14" (13–36 cm)

Flower: tight spike cluster, 1–3" (2.5–7.5 cm) long, of 10–20 yellow (can be maroon, red, white or bicolored) flowers; each flower, ¾" (2 cm) long, 2 petals (lips), upper lip forms a "hood" over shorter (sometimes white) lower lip; cluster looks fuzzy

Leaf: basal, narrow and fern-like, 2–6" (5–15 cm) long, highly lobed, wavy margins, covered with fine white hairs, long leafstalk; much shorter stem leaves

Bloom: summer

Cycle/Origin: perennial; native

Habitat: moist soils, open woods, ridges, slopes, meadows

Range: throughout

Notes: This native perennial spreads by short horizontal stems, often forming large patches. Flowers can be all yellow, all red or bicolored (yellow and red). The hairy leaves are often purplish and most rise from the base of the plant, but it also has several stem leaves. The plant is semiparasitic, obtaining some nutrients from the roots of other plants. Its genus name *Pedicularis* means "of lice." Called "lousewort" because it was once believed that if livestock ate the plant, they would become infested with lice. There are about 40 species of lousewort in North America. Ranges throughout the Carolinas, but rarely found near the Carolina coast.

CLUSTER TYPE
Spike

FLOWER TYPE
Irregular

LEAF TYPE
Simple Lobed

LEAF ATTACHMENT
Alternate

LEAF ATTACHMENT
Basal

St. Anthony's Turnip
Ranunculus bulbosus

Family: Buttercup (Ranunculaceae)

Height: 8–24" (20–61 cm)

Flower: bright yellow, 1½" (4 cm) wide, made up of 5 oval overlapping petals surrounding a mounded green-and-yellow center; downward-pointing, triangular, purple-tipped bracts beneath flower

Leaf: basal, compound, 2½–3" (6–7.5 cm) long, on long fleshy leafstalk, made up of 3 arrowhead-shaped leaflets with irregular lobes; a few scattered stem leaves (cauline) are lobed, alternately attached, smaller toward top of stem; branching, hollow, purplish stem has lengthwise furrows

Bloom: spring, summer

Cycle/Origin: perennial; non-native

Habitat: moist soils, old fields, lawns, meadows, disturbed sites, sun

Range: throughout

Notes: Originally from Europe, this weedy species has naturalized throughout much of the eastern U.S. and the western coastal states. Species name *bulbosus* refers to the bulbous base, which resembles the common garden turnip, thus the latter part of the common name. Distinguished from all other buttercup species by its enlarged base. The roots, when ground up and applied to the skin, will raise blisters and have been used to treat skin ailments such as shingles.

FLOWER TYPE
Regular

LEAF TYPE
Simple Lobed

LEAF TYPE
Compound

LEAF ATTACHMENT
Alternate

LEAF ATTACHMENT
Basal

Common Dandelion
Taraxacum officinale

Family: Aster (Asteraceae)

Height: 2–18" (5–45 cm)

Flower: yellow, 1½" (4 cm) wide; appears as 1 large flower, but is actually a composite of many tiny flowers that are clustered together

Leaf: lobed, 2–8" (5–20 cm) long, dark green, with deep lobes and sharp teeth, basally attached in a rosette

Bloom: year-round

Cycle/Origin: perennial; non-native

Habitat: dry soils, disturbed sites, lawns, fields, roadsides, along trails, sun

Range: throughout

Notes: A non-native perennial responsible for much water contamination, as people treat lawns with chemicals to eradicate Common Dandelion. In French, *dent-de-lion* refers to the toothed leaves, which resemble the teeth of a lion. Its flowers open in mornings and close in afternoons. The globe-like seed heads have soft hair-like bristles that resemble tiny parachutes, which carry the seeds away on the wind. Originally brought from Eurasia as a food crop. Its leaves are bitter, but offer high vitamin and mineral content. The long taproot has been roasted and ground to use as a coffee substitute.

FLOWER TYPE
Composite

LEAF TYPE
Simple Lobed

LEAF ATTACHMENT
Basal

Purplehead Sneezeweed

Helenium flexuosum

Family: Aster (Asteraceae)

Height: 8–36" (20–91 cm)

Flower: yellow flower head, 1½" (4 cm) wide, daisy-like, made up of 8–13 drooping petals (ray flowers) around a domed brownish purple center (disk flowers); each petal tip has 3 lobes

Leaf: basal, elliptical, 8" (20 cm) long; stem (cauline) leaf, smaller and lance-shaped, 1¼–4¾" (3–12 cm) long, alternately attached; the leaf base extends down the stem, forming distinctive wings; both types hairy and rough to the touch

Bloom: summer, fall

Cycle/Origin: perennial; native

Habitat: moist soils, ditches, riverbanks, open pinewoods

Range: throughout

Notes: A common weed of wet disturbed areas throughout the eastern U.S., Purplehead Sneezeweed is often seen growing alone in overgrazed pastures. Cows avoid eating the plant because it contains a poisonous compound, which is now being investigated for anticancer properties. Thus even a "lowly" weed may be valuable in unforeseen ways. Common Sneezeweed (pg. 369) is similar, but the center of its flower is distinctly ball-like and yellow-green, unlike the domed brownish purple center of Purplehead Sneezeweed.

FLOWER TYPE **Composite**   LEAF TYPE **Simple**   LEAF ATTACHMENT **Alternate**   LEAF ATTACHMENT **Basal**

Downy Yellow False Foxglove

Aureolaria virginica

Family: Snapdragon (Scrophulariaceae)

Height: 1–5' (30–152 cm)

Flower: spike cluster, 2–4" (5–10 cm) long, of buttery yellow flowers; each trumpet-shaped flower, 1½" (4 cm) long, made up of 5 petals fused to form a tube that flares at the mouth; cluster is at end of a single or sparsely branched stem

Leaf: upper, lance-shaped to oval, 2½–5" (6–13 cm) long, smooth margin; middle, slightly lobed; lower, lobed and appearing similar to oak leaves; all leaves are soft and hairy; hairy stem

Fruit: oval green pod, turning brown, 1½" (1 cm) long, covered with dense downy hairs

Bloom: summer

Cycle/Origin: perennial; native

Habitat: dry soils, edges of woods containing White Oaks, sun to partial shade

Range: throughout

Notes: Sometimes called Virginia Oak-leech, this semiparasitic flower gets part of its nutrients from the roots of White Oak trees. Because of this, it is always found within the drip line of the canopy of a White Oak. Four other species of yellow false foxglove bloom in the Carolinas. Bumblebees pollinate false foxgloves, entering them by backing into the trumpet-shaped flowers.

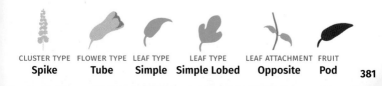

CLUSTER TYPE **Spike**   FLOWER TYPE **Tube**   LEAF TYPE **Simple**   LEAF TYPE **Simple Lobed**   LEAF ATTACHMENT **Opposite**   FRUIT **Pod**

Sweetclover

Melilotus officinalis

Family: Pea or Bean (Fabaceae)

Height: 3–6' (.9–1.8 m)

Flower: spike cluster, 1½–4¾" (4–12 cm) long, of yellow flowers; each flower, ¼" (.6 cm) long

Leaf: compound, made up of 3 narrow lance-shaped leaflets; each leaflet, ½–1" (1–2.5 cm) long, toothed; leaves alternately attached to branching stem

Fruit: egg-shaped green pod, turning brown, ¼" (.6 cm) long, flattened

Bloom: spring, summer, fall

Cycle/Origin: annual, biennial; non-native

Habitat: wet or dry soils, roadsides, along railroads, open fields, waste areas, sun

Range: throughout

Notes: This non-native plant was introduced from Europe via Eurasia. Once grown as a hay crop, it has escaped cultivation and now grows throughout the Carolinas along roads and fields. When crushed, the leaves and flowers smell like vanilla. Appropriately in the genus *Melilotus*, which is Greek for "honey," as bees produce honey from the nectar of this plant. Leaves are eaten by White-tailed Deer. The rodenticide warfarin was developed from the chemical dicoumarin, found in sweet clover.

CLUSTER TYPE	FLOWER TYPE	LEAF TYPE	LEAF ATTACHMENT	LEAF ATTACHMENT	FRUIT
Spike	**Irregular**	**Compound**	**Alternate**	**Basal**	**Pod**

Carolina Desert-chicory

Pyrrhopappus carolinianus

Family: Aster (Asteraceae)

Height: 8–36" (20–91 cm)

Flower: bright yellow flower head, 2" (5 cm) wide, dandelion-like, made up of narrow oblong petals (ray flowers) with fringed tips; pointed vase-shaped green bracts clasp flower head; flower on long slender stalk; 1 to several flower heads per plant

Leaf: basal, dandelion-like, 3–10" (7.5–25 cm) long, edges with small irregular teeth or deeply lobed with a few long irregular narrow projections; basal leaves form a dense rosette; few stem leaves are alternately attached; smooth or slightly hairy stem

Bloom: spring, summer

Cycle/Origin: annual, biennial; native

Habitat: dry soils, open woods, disturbed areas, lawns, sun

Range: throughout the Carolinas, except in the westernmost counties of North Carolina

Notes: Sweat bees, the main pollinator of this early morning bloom, tear open the anthers and remove the pollen before other bees become active. Also called False Dandelion because it looks similar to Common Dandelion (pg. 377), but it is taller than Common Dandelion and has leaves on its stems. Stems exude a milky sap when broken or cut. Sometimes called Texas Dandelion, possibly for its "Texas-sized" flower heads.

FLOWER TYPE	LEAF TYPE	LEAF TYPE	LEAF ATTACHMENT	LEAF ATTACHMENT
Composite	**Simple**	**Simple Lobed**	**Alternate**	**Basal**

Greater Tickseed
Coreopsis major

Family: Aster (Asteraceae)

Height: 24–36" (61–91 cm)

Flower: large bright yellow flower head, 2½" (6 cm) wide, made up of 6–10 (usually 8) slim petals (ray flowers) widely spaced around reddish yellow center (disk flowers); ray flowers have a few red spots

Leaf: compound, made up of 3 leaflets; each lance-shaped leaflet, 1–3" (2.5–7.5 cm) long, smooth margin; leaves are stalkless, oppositely attached, forming an apparent whorl of 6 leaflets around a fuzzy green stem

Bloom: spring, summer, fall

Cycle/Origin: perennial; native

Habitat: dry soils, woods, thickets, fields, disturbed areas, sandhills, sun

Range: throughout

Notes: Also commonly called Whorlleaf Coreopsis since the plant appears to have whorls of six leaflets (making it easy to identify), but the compound leaves are actually oppositely attached. This is a beautiful cheery blossom that attracts butterflies and is frequently cultivated in wildflower gardens. The North Carolina Department of Transportation uses two relatives also in the *Coreopsis* genus, Lanceleaf Tickseed (*C. lanceolata*) and Golden Tickseed (*C. tinctoria*) (neither shown), in highway plantings.

FLOWER TYPE
Composite

LEAF TYPE
Compound

LEAF ATTACHMENT
Opposite

Black-eyed Susan

Rudbeckia hirta

Family: Aster (Asteraceae)

Height: 12–36" (30–91 cm)

Flower: yellow flower head, 2–3" (5–7.5 cm) wide, daisy-like, composed of 10–20 petals (ray flowers) around a raised button-like brown center (disk flowers); 1 to numerous large flower heads per plant

Leaf: slender, lance-shaped or elliptical, 2–7" (5–18 cm) long, very hairy, toothless, alternately attached; winged leafstalk clasps a hairy stem

Bloom: summer

Cycle/Origin: annual, perennial, biennial; native

Habitat: dry soils, open woods, disturbed areas, sun

Range: throughout

Notes: Also called Brown-eyed Susan, but just who "Susan" was remains unknown. A native that is also widely cultivated and now found in just about any habitat. Look for three prominent veins on each leaf and a characteristic winged leafstalk clasping each erect straight stem. Species name *hirta* is Latin for "hairy" or "rough" and refers to the plant's hairy stems and leaves. Seeds are an abundant food source for small mammals and songbirds, and the flowers attract butterflies. Close relatives Orange Coneflower (*R. fulgida)* and Thinleaf Coneflower (*R. triloba*) (neither shown) are similar, but bloom in late summer and in fall.

FLOWER TYPE | LEAF TYPE | LEAF ATTACHMENT | LEAF ATTACHMENT
Composite | **Simple** | **Alternate** | **Clasping**

Bearded Beggartick
Bidens aristosa

Family: Aster (Asteraceae)

Height: 1–5' (30–152 cm)

Flower: bright yellow flower head, 2–3" (5–7.5 cm) wide, made up of 8 petals (ray flowers) and a tall yellow and brown center (disk flowers); flower heads on long stalks at ends of multi-branched stem

Leaf: compound (may be twice compound), 5–15" (13–38 cm) long, made up of lance-shaped leaflets; each leaflet, coarsely toothed, opposite; dark green leaves are alternately attached along the reddish stem

Bloom: late summer, fall

Cycle/Origin: annual, biennial; native

Habitat: wet soils, ditches, marshes, meadows, roadsides, forest edges, sun

Range: throughout

Notes: Most common in the hills and plains of the Carolinas, Bearded Beggartick flowers create spectacular displays along roads when blooming in late summer and in autumn. Despite its tendency to become an invasive weed, the North Carolina Department of Transportation plants it along highways. The flower head looks like a sunflower, but true sunflowers do not have compound leaves. Its small flattened seeds have two barbs. After the seeds ripen in November, they are often found "hitching a ride" on the clothing of hikers, thus "Beggartick" in the common name.

FLOWER TYPE
Composite

LEAF TYPE
Compound

LEAF TYPE
Twice Compound

LEAF ATTACHMENT
Alternate

LEAF ATTACHMENT
Basal

Swamp Sunflower
Helianthus angustifolius

Family: Aster (Asteraceae)

Height: 2–5' (61–152 cm)

Flower: bright yellow flower head, 2–3" (5–7.5 cm) wide, made up of 10–15 petals (ray flowers) and a darker center (disk flowers)

Leaf: basal, very narrow, 2–6" (5–15 cm) long, dark green and rough with middle vein depressed above, lighter green with fine hairs and middle vein raised below, pointed tip, mostly stalkless, smooth margin rolled under; numerous stem leaves

Bloom: summer, fall

Cycle/Origin: perennial; native

Habitat: wet soils, swamps, coastal salt marshes, roadsides

Range: eastern half of the Carolinas

Notes: Also called Narrowleaf Sunflower for its very slim leaves. Swamp Sunflower is a good plant for coastal wildflower gardens as it tolerates salty boggy soils, but it also adapts to drier conditions. It attracts fall butterflies to its nectar and goldfinches to its seed. The seeds are sown along highways by the North Carolina Department of Transportation. The Woodland Sunflower (*H. divaricatus*) (not shown), a relative that can be differentiated from Swamp Sunflower by its yellow center and broad opposite leaves, is scattered throughout the Carolinas in large colonies.

FLOWER TYPE
Composite

LEAF TYPE
Simple

LEAF ATTACHMENT
Alternate

LEAF ATTACHMENT
Basal

Early Yellowrocket

Barbarea verna

Family: Mustard (Brassicaceae)

Height: 12–36" (30–91 cm)

Flower: spike cluster, 2–3" (5–7.5 cm) wide, of numerous, bright yellow flowers; each small tubular flower, ½" (1 cm) wide, 4 petals fused to form a tube; 1 cluster at end of each of the multiple branches of stem

Leaf: basal, oblong and lobed, 8½" (22 cm) long, 4–10 pair of deep lobes with wavy margins; stem leaf smaller, 3-8 pair of lobes with smooth margins

Fruit: narrow erect greenish pod, turning tan to brown, 2–3" (5–7.5 cm) long, splits lengthwise into 2 curled sides to release many tiny black seeds

Bloom: spring, summer

Cycle/Origin: perennial, biennial; non-native

Habitat: moist soils, disturbed areas, sun

Range: throughout

Notes: Introduced from Europe and Asia and still cultivated in Europe, Early Yellowrocket is now a common weed across most of the eastern third of the United States and in a few western states. One of the earliest sprouting wildflowers of spring in the East. The new foliage was eagerly anticipated by the early settlers, who ate it raw in salads or cooked as greens, boiling it twice in water to remove the bitter taste.

CLUSTER TYPE	FLOWER TYPE	LEAF TYPE	LEAF ATTACHMENT	LEAF ATTACHMENT	FRUIT
Spike	**Tube**	**Simple Lobed**	**Alternate**	**Basal**	**Pod**

Yellow Pitcherplant
Sarracenia flava

Family: Pitcher Plant (Sarraceniaceae)

Height: 12–36" (30–91 cm)

Flower: yellow (rarely red), 3–4" (7.5–10 cm) wide, droops from a single tall leafless stalk; 5 flat long belt-like petals dangling below 5 bluntly triangular green or yellow sepals; flower smells like cat urine

Leaf: stalkless, 12–36" (30–91 cm) long, forming tall slender tube flaring at top and rolling under to form narrow rim, pinching in on 1 side to form "neck," then widening again into a "hood" that arches over the hollow tube

Bloom: spring, summer, fall

Cycle/Origin: perennial; native

Habitat: wet acid soils, sandy bogs, pinelands, ditches, sun

Range: eastern half of the Carolinas

Notes: Carnivorous, the Yellow Pitcherplant relies on insects to supplement needed nutrients (especially nitrogen) not accessible in bog soils. Oddly, the leaf produces insect-attracting nectar at the rim and just under the "hood." Insects slip on a waxy substance coating the inside of the leaf, falling into rainwater held by the "pitcher." The leaf secretes a wetting agent and enzymes into the water, causing insects to drown quickly and dissolve and allowing the plant to absorb the nutrients. Leaf color varies widely. Leaves can be red, red-veined, green with a red throat, all yellowish green or all yellow.

FLOWER TYPE
Irregular

LEAF TYPE
Simple Lobed

LEAF ATTACHMENT
Basal

Canada Goldenrod
Solidago canadensis

Family: Aster (Asteraceae)

Height: 2–7' (.6–2.1 m)

Flower: mass of large arching spike clusters, 3–9" (7.5–23 cm) long; each spike made up of yellow flower heads; each flower head, ¼" (.6 cm) wide; the tip of each spike usually nods to 1 side

Leaf: narrow, lance-shaped, 1¼–6" (3–15 cm) long, rough upper surface, shallow sharp teeth, stalkless; fewer leaves toward stem base; stem branches near top

Bloom: fall

Cycle/Origin: perennial; native

Habitat: dry soils, disturbed areas, open woods, sun

Range: throughout

Notes: This common plant was named South Carolina's state wildflower in 2003. Also called Late Goldenrod, Common Goldenrod or Field Goldenrod. Often seen at roadsides in patches 8–30 feet (2.4–9.1 m) wide, excluding other plants from the site. The more than 50 species of goldenrod in the Carolinas are difficult to positively identify from one another. While most fall-blooming yellow flowers are goldenrods, which are often blamed for hay fever, autumn allergies are actually caused mainly by Ragweed (*Ambrosia artemisiifolia*) (not shown). Only 1–2 percent of fall airborne pollen is from goldenrod.

CLUSTER TYPE	FLOWER TYPE	LEAF TYPE	LEAF ATTACHMENT
Spike	**Composite**	**Simple**	**Alternate**

Jerusalem Artichoke

Helianthus tuberosus

Family: Aster (Asteraceae)

Height: 3–10' (.9–3 m)

Flower: yellow flower head, 3½–6" (9–15 cm) wide, made up of 10–20 petals (ray flowers) and a brownish yellow center (disk flowers)

Leaf: broadly lance-shaped, 4–10" (10–25 cm) long, toothed margin, rough upper surface; numerous leaves alternately attached on upper two-thirds of stem, oppositely attached on lower third; sturdy, hairy, multi-branched green stem

Bloom: summer, fall

Cycle/Origin: perennial; non-native

Habitat: dry soils, pastures, disturbed sites, roadsides, hay fields, gardens, woods, sun

Range: throughout

Notes: "Artichoke" in the common name of this sunflower is for its edible roots, which are often used in place of potatoes in recipes. Some people think the roots taste like the common artichoke. The knobby tubers have a pinkish skin and are concentrated at the base of the stem. American Indians cultivated it as a staple crop for centuries prior to the arrival of the settlers. Introduced to the Carolinas from the western United States and now a common garden plant across this country and in England. This non-native plant has much broader leaves than those of native sunflowers in the Carolinas.

FLOWER TYPE
Composite

LEAF TYPE
Simple

LEAF ATTACHMENT
Alternate

LEAF ATTACHMENT
Opposite

Horseflyweed
Baptisia tinctoria

Family: Pea or Bean (Fabaceae)

Height: 12–36" (30–91 cm)

Flower: spike cluster, 4–5" (10–13 cm) long, of small pea-like, bright yellow-to-cream flowers; each flower, ½" (1 cm) long; flowers are horizontal to and sparsely arranged on 1 side of stem

Leaf: compound, 3-parted and clover-like; each tear-drop-shaped leaflet, ½–1" (1–2.5 cm) long, bluish green, stalkless; yellowish green (dotted with black) stem is widely branched and smooth

Fruit: globular dark bluish green pod, turning bluish black, ½" (1 cm) long

Bloom: summer, fall

Cycle/Origin: perennial; native

Habitat: dry sandy soils, woods, old fields, sun to part shade

Range: throughout

Notes: All plant parts turn black when dried, indicative of the blue dye inside, which was once used to color cloth. Proven to improve the body's immune system and its ability to fight bacteria and toxins. Recent increased medicinal use has reduced its numbers to critical levels in some states. Grayhairy Wild Indigo (pg. 405) is similar, but has larger flowers, hairs pressed closely to the stem and occurs only in the eastern Carolinas. Also known as Yellow Wild Indigo.

CLUSTER TYPE	FLOWER TYPE	LEAF TYPE	LEAF ATTACHMENT	FRUIT
Spike	**Irregular**	**Compound**	**Alternate**	**Pod**

Grayhairy Wild Indigo
Baptisia cinerea

Family: Pea or Bean (Fabaceae)

Height: 12–24" (30–61 cm)

Flower: spike cluster, 4–8" (10–20 cm) long, of large pea-like yellow flowers; each flower, ¾–1" (2–2.5 cm) long; 1 to a few spikes per plant

Leaf: compound, made up 3 leaflets; each oval leaflet, 1½–3¼" (4–8 cm) long, leathery, widest at tip; leaves on long stalks; hairy stem

Fruit: pea-like green pod, turning nearly black, ¾–1½" (2–3 cm) long, flattened

Bloom: spring, summer

Cycle/Origin: perennial; native

Habitat: dry sandy soils, Longleaf Pine woods, partial sun

Range: eastern half of the Carolinas

Notes: Common along the coast and in the sandhills, this large-flowered member of the Pea or Bean family is one of the indicators of pinewoods in the Carolinas. This plant is native to only a narrow area along the coast, stretching from southern Virginia to southern South Carolina. It is named for the gray hairs pressed closely along the purplish green stem. Species name *cinerea* is Latin and means "ashy," referring to color of the leaves in winter. The leaves stay on the plant in winter, but turn ashy gray, as does the stem. Related to Horseflyweed (pg. 403), which has smooth stems and smaller leaflets, flowers and fruit.

CLUSTER TYPE
Spike

FLOWER TYPE
Irregular

LEAF TYPE
Compound

LEAF ATTACHMENT
Alternate

FRUIT
Pod

fruit

Showy Rattlebox
Crotalaria spectabilis

Family: Pea or Bean (Fabaceae)

Height: 2–4' (61–122 cm)

Flower: spike cluster, 4–12" (10–30 cm) long, of many large pea-like, bright yellow flowers; each flower, 1" (2.5 cm) long, dangling on short stalk

Leaf: oblong and lance-shaped, 2–6" (5–15 cm) long, alternately attached

Fruit: bulging oval green pod, turning tan, then black, 1–1½" (2.5–4 cm) long, black seeds inside pod dry and loosen when mature and rattle when the pod is disturbed

Bloom: summer, fall

Cycle/Origin: annual; non-native

Habitat: sandy soils, disturbed areas, old pastures, sun

Range: eastern half of the Carolinas

Notes: Showy Rattlebox was introduced from India to restore nitrogen and humus to farmlands. Now considered an invasive weed in agricultural areas. All parts of this legume are poisonous to humans and livestock. Less invasive native relatives, Rabbitbells (*C. rotundifolia*) and Pursh Rattlebox (*C. purshii*) (neither shown), share the range of Showy Rattlebox. All three species have pea-like yellow flowers, but Showy Rattlebox has larger flowers than the other two, Rabbitbells has nearly round leaves and the leaves of Pursh Rattlebox are compound.

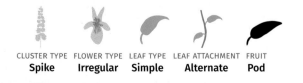

CLUSTER TYPE	FLOWER TYPE	LEAF TYPE	LEAF ATTACHMENT	FRUIT
Spike	**Irregular**	**Simple**	**Alternate**	**Pod**

Common Evening Primrose
Oenothera biennis

Family: Evening Primrose (Onagraceae)

Height: 2–5' (61–152 cm)

Flower: loose round cluster, 6–10" (15–25 cm) wide, made up of many pale yellow flowers; each flower, 1–2" (2.5–5 cm) wide, made up of 4 petals and an X-shaped center (stigma)

Leaf: narrowly lance-shaped, 4–8" (10–20 cm) long, rough to the touch, red-tinged margin; alternately attached along a hairy, reddish green stem

Fruit: blunt-topped cylindrical green pod, turning brown, ½–2" (1–5 cm) long, lengthwise ridges

Bloom: summer, fall

Cycle/Origin: biennial; native

Habitat: dry soils, fields, thickets, disturbed areas, sun

Range: throughout

Notes: A biennial, producing a low ring (rosette) of leaves in its first year, sending up a tall flower stalk in the second. The flowers bloom from the bottom of the cluster up, opening a few at a time. Flowers open in the evening (hence the common name) and last until about noon the next day before wilting. Pollinated at night by Sphinx Moths. Pods contain many seeds and are eaten by wildlife. About 150 species in the *Oenothera* genus in the Western Hemisphere, with about 15 Evening Primrose species found in the Carolinas.

CLUSTER TYPE **Round** FLOWER TYPE **Regular** LEAF TYPE **Simple** LEAF ATTACHMENT **Alternate** FRUIT **Pod**

Gray Goldenrod
Solidago nemoralis

Family: Aster (Asteraceae)

Height: 12–36" (30–91 cm)

Flower: nodding spike cluster, 8" (20 cm) long, made up of 10–20 small yellow flower heads; each flower head, ¼" (.6 cm) wide, densely arranged on 1 side of fine-haired grayish or reddish stem

Leaf: basal, oval, 2–4¾" (5–12 cm) long, grayish green, tapering at base, coarse-toothed margin toward tip, fine dense hairs; stem leaf, narrowly oval, tapering at both ends, smooth margin

Bloom: fall

Cycle/Origin: perennial; native

Habitat: old fields, eroded hillsides, woodlands, sun

Range: throughout

Notes: Gray Goldenrod looks similar to the more than 50 other species of goldenrod in the Carolinas. Commonly found in worn-out pastures, hence another common name, Old Field Goldenrod. The North Carolina Department of Transportation plants it along highways. This wildflower is a good choice for butterfly gardens with rocky or poor soils. A variety of insects such as butterflies, moths, bees, wasps, flies and beetles visit the flowers for the pollen and nectar, and the seeds are eaten by American Goldfinches. Also known as Dyer's Weed, the flowers produce a yellow dye used by basket and textile weavers.

CLUSTER TYPE **Spike** FLOWER TYPE **Composite** LEAF TYPE **Simple** LEAF ATTACHMENT **Alternate** LEAF ATTACHMENT **Basal**

411

Yellow Crownbeard
Verbesina occidentalis

Family: Aster (Asteraceae)

Height: 7–10' (2.1–3 m)

Flower: ragged flat cluster, 10–12" (25–30 cm) wide, of yellow flower heads; each flower head, 2–2½" (5–6 cm) wide, made of 2–5 petals (ray flowers) unevenly spaced around yellow center (disk flowers)

Leaf: broadly lance-shaped, 3–8" (7.5–20 cm) long, small-toothed margin, oppositely attached; long leafstalk extends down stem, forming wings; erect (usually unbranched) stem

Bloom: summer, fall

Cycle/Origin: perennial; native

Habitat: moist soils, disturbed ground, pastures, roadsides, fencerows, hay fields, river edges, forest edges, sun to partial sun

Range: throughout

Notes: The North Carolina Department of Transportation seeds Yellow Crownbeard and the similar Wingstem (*V. alternifolia*) (not shown) along highways. Ranging in the western half of North Carolina, Wingstem differs from Yellow Crownbeard by having alternately attached leaves. Both species have wide wings on the stems formed by the leafstalks. Yellow Crownbeard occurs in large dense masses, often under trees or filling old fields. Its foliage is food for Pearl Crescent and Bordered Patch butterfly caterpillars.

CLUSTER TYPE **Flat**   FLOWER TYPE **Composite**   LEAF TYPE **Simple**   LEAF ATTACHMENT **Opposite**

flower

Small's Ragwort

Packera anonyma

Family: Aster (Asteraceae)

Height: 12–36" (30–91 cm)

Flower: disk-shaped flat cluster, 10–20" (25–50 cm) wide, of daisy-like, golden yellow flower heads; each flower head, ⅝" (1.5 cm) wide, made up of 8–13 petals (ray flowers) surrounding a raised button-like center of densely packed, orangish yellow disk flowers; 20–100 flower heads per plant

Leaf: basal, oval, 1½–6" (4–15 cm) long, pointed tip, blunt-toothed margin, long stalk; stem leaf, lance-shaped, deeply lobed with sharp teeth; stem has web-like dense white hairs at base

Bloom: spring, summer

Cycle/Origin: perennial; native

Habitat: dry soils, old pastures, near granite hillocks, sun

Range: throughout

Notes: Evergreen, this common perennial weed has a rosette of long-stalked leaves most of the year. One of the few spring bloomers among the multitude of yellow composite flowers, which botanists sometimes call DYCs or "darn yellow composites" because they are difficult to distinguish from one another. Also called Appalachian Ragwort. The flowers attract many butterfly species, and the caterpillars of some of those species eat the leaves.

CLUSTER TYPE
Flat

FLOWER TYPE
Composite

LEAF TYPE
Simple

LEAF TYPE
Simple Lobed

LEAF ATTACHMENT
Alternate

LEAF ATTACHMENT
Basal

flower

Common Mullein
Verbascum thapsus

Family: Snapdragon (Scrophulariaceae)

Height: 2–6' (.6–1.8 m)

Flower: club-like spike cluster, 12–24" (30–61 cm) long, of many small yellow flowers; each flower, ¾–1" (2–2.5 cm) wide, with 5 petals; flowers are packed along the stalk and open only a few at a time, from the top down

Leaf: large lower, 12–15" (30–38 cm) long, velvety with thick covering of stiff hairs; upper, stalkless, alternately attached, clasps the main stem; leaves progressively smaller toward top of stalk

Bloom: summer, fall

Cycle/Origin: biennial; non-native

Habitat: dry soils, fields, along roads, disturbed sites, sun

Range: throughout

Notes: A European import known for its very soft, flannel-like leaves, hence its other common name, Flannel Plant. This biennial takes two years to mature. The first year it grows as a low rosette of large soft leaves; in the second, a tall flower stalk sprouts. Its dried stems stand well into winter. It is said the Romans dipped its dried flower stalks in animal tallow to use as torches. Victorian women rubbed the leaves on their cheeks, slightly irritating their skin, to add a dash of blush. Early settlers and American Indians placed the soft woolly leaves in footwear for warmth and comfort.

CLUSTER TYPE	FLOWER TYPE	LEAF TYPE	LEAF ATTACHMENT	LEAF ATTACHMENT	LEAF ATTACHMENT
Spike	**Regular**	**Simple**	**Alternate**	**Basal**	**Clasping**

CHECKLIST/INDEX BY SPECIES

Use the boxes to check the flowers you've seen.

GLOSSARY

Alternate: A type of leaf attachment where the leaves are singly and alternately attached along the stem, not paired or in whorls.

Annual: A plant that germinates, flowers and sets seed during a single growing season and returns the following year only from seed.

Anther: A part of the male flower that contains the pollen.

Axil: The angle formed between a stem and a leafstalk.

Axis: A point on the main stem from which lateral branches arise.

Basal: Leaves at the base of a plant, near the ground, usually grouped in a round rosette.

Bell flower: A single downward-hanging flower with petals fused together that form a bell-like shape.

Berry: A fleshy fruit containing one or many seeds (e.g., a grape or tomato).

Biennial: A plant that lives for only two years, and blooms in the second year.

Bract: A leaf-like structure usually found at the base of a flower, often appearing as a petal.

Bulb: A short, round, underground shoot used as a food storage system, common in the Onion family.

Calyx: The name for the collective group of all of the sepals of a flower.

Cauline: Leaves that attach to the stem distinctly above the ground, as opposed to basal leaves that attach near the ground.

Clasping: A type of leaf attachment where the leaf base partly surrounds the plant's main stem at the point of attachment; the leaf grasps the stem without a leafstalk.

Cluster: A group or collection of flowers or leaves.

Composite flower: A collection of tiny flowers that appear as one large flower. Usually made up of ray and disk flowers, pertaining to members of the Aster family (e.g., common daisy).

Compound leaf: A single leaf composed of a central stalk and two or more leaflets.

Coniferous: Plants that do not shed their leaves each autumn (e.g., pine and spruce).

Corm: A short, thickened, vertical, underground stem used to store food.

Deciduous: Plants that shed their leaves each autumn (e.g., maples and oaks).

Disk flower: The small tubular flowers in the central part of a composite flower in the Aster family, such as the center of a daisy.

Ephemeral: Lasting for only a short time each spring.

Flat cluster: A group of flowers that form a flat-topped structure, which enables insects to easily land and thereby complete pollination; exhibited by plants of the Carrot family (e.g., Queen Anne's Lace).

Gland: A tiny structure, usually secreting oil or nectar, sometimes found on leaves, stems, stalks and flowers, such as in Gumweed.

Irregular flower: A flower that does not have the typical round shape, usually made up of 5 or more petals that are fused together in an irregular shape (e.g., pea or bean flower).

Leaflet: One of many leaf-like parts of a compound leaf. A compound leaf is made up of two or more leaflets.

Lip: The projection of a flower petal, or the "odd" petal, such as the large inflated petal of an orchid; may also refer to the lobes of a petal.

Lobed: A simple leaf with one or more indentations (sinuses) along its edge that do not reach the center or base of the leaf, (e.g., dandelion or oak leaf).

Margin: The edge of a leaf.

Mycorrhiza: A mutually beneficial relationship between a fungus and the root system of a plant.

Node: The place or point of origin on a stem where leaves attach (or have been attached).

Opposite leaves: A type of leaf attachment where the leaves are situated directly across the stem from each other.

Palmate: A type of compound leaf where three or more leaflets arise from a common central point which is at the end of a leafstalk, such as in Wild Lupine.

Parasitic: A plant or fungus that derives its food or water chiefly from another plant, to the detriment of the host plant.

Perennial: A plant that lives from several to many seasons, returning each year from its roots.

Perfoliate: A type of leaf attachment where the base of a leaf is connected around the main stem so that the stem appears to pass through the stalkless leaf (e.g., Boneset).

Petal: A basic flower part, usually brightly colored, serving to attract pollinating insects.

Pistil: The female part of a flower made up of an ovary, style and stigma, often in the center of a flower.

Pod: A dry fruit that contains many seeds (e.g., a pea pod).

Pollination: The transfer of pollen from the male anther to the female stigma, resulting in the production of seeds.

Ray flowers: One of many individual outer flowers of a composite flower in the Aster family (e.g., a single petal of a daisy flower).

Regular flower: A flower with 3–20 typical petals arranged in a circle.

Rhizome: A creeping, underground, horizontal stem.

Rosette: A cluster of leaves arranged in a circle, often at the base of the plant, as in Common Mullein.

Round cluster: A group of many flowers that form a round structure, giving the appearance of one large flower.

Saprophytic: A plant or fungus that lives on dead organic (plant) matter, neither parasitic nor making its own food (e.g., Indian Pipe).

Seed head: A group or cluster of seeds.

Sepal: A member of the outermost set of petals of a flower, typically green or leafy but often colored and resembling a petal (e.g., lily).

Sheath: A tubular leaf-like structure that surrounds the stem (e.g., Spotted Coralroot).

Simple leaf: A single leaf with an undivided or unlobed edge.

Spadix: A highly specialized, thickened spike with many small flowers that are crowded together (e.g., Jack-in-the-pulpit). See spathe.

Spathe: A large, usually solitary, petal-like bract often enclosing a group of flowers, such as a spadix (e.g., Jack-in-the-pulpit). See spadix.

Spike cluster: Many flowers on a single spike-like stem, giving the appearance of one large flower.

Spur: A hollow, tube-like appendage of a flower, usually where nectar is located (e.g., Jewelweed).

Stamen: Collectively, the male parts of a flower consisting of an anther and filament.

Stem leaf: Any leaf that is found along a plant's stem, as opposed to a leaf at the base of a plant (basal). See cauline.

Stigma: The female part of the flower that receives the pollen.

Stipules: A pair of basal appendages of a leaf, not attached to the leaf blade.

Stolon: A creeping stem on the surface of ground (e.g., Creeping Charlie).

Toothed: The jagged or serrated edge of a leaf, resembling the teeth of a saw.

Tube flower: Similar to a bell flower with fused petals that form a tube, usually turned upward, not hanging downward.

Whorled: A circle or ring of three or more similar leaves, stems or flowers originating from a common point.

Wing: A flat extension at the base of a leaf or edge of a leafstalk, sometimes extending down the stem of the plant.

Woody: Stems that are hard and brown, usually with bark; not a soft green stem.

NOTES

NOTES

NOTES

NOTES

PHOTO CREDITS, CONT.

All photos are copyright of their respective photographers.

Mrs. W.D. Bransford/Lady Bird Johnson Wildflower Center: 122; **Katy Chayka:** 322; **Shirley Denton:** 398; **Frank Duton/www.Toledo-Bend.us:** 326 (flower inset); **Dudley Edmondson:** 162, 236, 346; **Chris Evans:** 174; **Erv Evans:** 70, 116, 132; **Gary P. Flemming/Virginia Natural Heritage Program:** 298, 402; **Glen Galau:** 226; **Denise Greene:** 94 (fruit inset); **Mike Haddock:** 278; **Jesse Harris:** 182, 326 (main), 352, 384, 404; **Richard Haug:** 128; **Jason M. Hogle:** 82; **Jerry and Barbara Jividen:** 118 (main); **William S. Justice/Smithsonian Institute:** 84, 164, 348 (main); **Bert Katzung:** 306; **T. Beth Kinsey:** 178, 314 (fruit inset); **Kathryn Kirk:** 114 (fruit inset); **Louis-M. Landry:** 280; **Linda Lee/University of South Carolina Herbarium:** 68, 88, 90, 136, 146, 154, 250, 276, 286, 328 (both), 336 (main), 344, 350, 386, 406; **Don Mammoser:** 244 (fruit inset); **Jim Manhart, Ph. D.:** 96 (fruit inset), 190; **Rick Mark:** 390; **David R. McAdoo:** 282 (both); **Tim McDowell:** 46 (main); **Steve Mortensen:** 208 (main); **Janet Novak:** 94 (main); **W. E. Ottinger:** 140; **Jeffrey S. Pippen:** 54, 144, 192, 194, 196, 224, 232, 300 (flower inset), 412; **Plant Delights Nursery, Inc.:** 130; **Ken Robertson/Illinois Natural History Survey:** 114 (main); **Alan Stenz/Missouri Botanical Garden PlantFinder:** 106 (fruit inset); **Janice Stiefel:** 160; **Stan Tekiela:** 22, 24, 30, 32, 40 (both), 48 (both), 52 (fruit inset), 58 (fruit inset), 62 (both), 158, 200, 214 (fruit inset), 230 (single inset), 244 (main), 254, 294, 296 (main), 302 (both), 308 (both), 310 (both), 368, 372 (main), 382, 416 (flower inset); **Connie Toops:** 320 (both); **James Van Kley:** 342; and **www.delawarewildflowers.org:** 268, 336 (fruit inset).

Images used under license from Shutterstock.com:
aga7ta: 400; **alybaba:** 348 (flower inset); **Amanda Feltz:** 56; **Andrea j Smith:** 312 (main); **aniana:** 202; **Ashley Keller:** 148; **Beach Creatives:** 260 (main), 292; **beckysphotos:** 220; **Bildagentur Zoonar GmbH:** 246; **CampSmoke:** 152; **Celine Kwang:** 92; **Conrad Barrington:** 58 (main); **Cynthia Shirk:** 53 (main); **Dan4Earth:** 234 (fruit inset), 258; **F_studio:** 222; **fedsax:** 416 (main); **Francisco Herrera:** 172 (main); **Frank Reiser:** 270; **Gerry Bishop:** 138, 208 (fruit inset), 210, 230 (main), 238, 372 (inset); **Gert-Jan van Vilet:** 42; **High Mountain:** 34; **homi:** 186 (both); **ImageNature:** 204 (main); **J Need:** 206; **J Wheeler:** 72; **Jacqueline F Cooper:** 110; **jadimages:** 108; **JayL:** 102; **Jeff Holcombe:** 300 (main), 338; **Joe Ferrer:** 408; **Josie Elias:** 170; **The Jungle Explorer:** 354; **K Hanley CHDPhoto:** 360; **karen burgess:** 256; **Kathy Clark:** 46 (fruit inset); **Kenneth Keifer:** 168 (both); **Kevin Collison:** 76; **krolya25:** 180 (main); **LEAF87:** 388; **Lesia Kapinosova:** 214 (main); **LFRabanedo:** 112; **Malachi Jacobs:** 74, 124; **MargareeClareys:** 106 (main); **Martin Fowler:** 198; **MaryAnne Campbell:** 240; **Matt Hopkins:** 212; **Melinda Fawver:** 28, 126; **meunierd:** 216; **Michael G McKinne:** 358; **Mira Drozdowski:** 26; **Mircea Costina:** 86; **Nahhana:** 100 (fruit inset), 340, 370; **NatalieSchorr:** 296 (fruit inset); **Nikolay Kurzenko:** 166; **Niliane Fatima Pierok:** 376; **Ole Schoener:** 98; **Ollga P:** 252; **OrelImages:** 362; **Orest Iyzhechka:** 284, 356; **Paul Bryan:** 67; **Sibirin:** 80; **simona pavan:** 264, 266, 374; **Starover Sibiriak:** 18; **Sunny Forest:** 64; **TreesG Photography:** 96 (main); **Vankich1:** 100 (main); **Victoria Tucholka:** 204 (flower inset); **zprecech:** 248; and **zzz555zzz:** 14.

These images are used under Attribution 2.0 Generic (CC BY 2.0) license, which can be found at https://creativecommons.org/licenses/by/2.0/: **Bobistraveling:** 184, no modifications, original image at https://www.flickr.com/photos/bobistraveling/9144638423/; **Doug McGrady:** 172 (yellow flower inset) , no modifications, original image at https://www.flickr.com/photos/douglas_mcgrady/36105191665; 272, no modifications, original image at https://www.flickr.com/photos/douglas_mcgrady/33814958143; **Wendell Smith:** 260 (ripe inset), no modifications, original image at https://www.flickr.com/photos/wendellsmith/9054158058/; 260 (unripe inset), no modifications, original image at https://www.flickr.com/photos/wendellsmith/9051929033/; **Superior National Forest:** 288, no modifications, original image at https://www.flickr.com/photos/superiornationalforest/5097903790/